IT'S ALL IN YOUR HEAD, M

Manjiri Indurkar writes from Jabalpur. She is one of the founders of the Bookshelf Writing Workshop. Her chapbook of poetry *Dental Hygiene is Very Important* was published in 2017. Her works have appeared in places like the *Indian Quarterly, Cha: Asian Literary Journal, Scroll,* the *Indian Express, Poetry at Sangam, Arre, The Bombay Literary Magazine, Himal, Skin Stories, Indian Cultural Forum,* and elsewhere.

it's all in your head, m

MANJIRI INDURKAR

First published by Tranquebar, an imprint of Westland Publications Private Limited, in 2020

1st Floor, A Block, East Wing, Plot No. 40, SP Infocity, Dr MGR Salai, Perungudi, Kandanchavadi, Chennai 600096

Westland, the Westland logo, Tranquebar and the Tranquebar logo are the trademarks of Westland Publications Private Limited, or its affi liates.

Copyright © Manjiri Indurkar, 2020

ISBN: 9789389648607

Typeset by R. Ajith Kumar

For Aai who doesn't know,
for Aaji who does,
for Baba who would rather not

Preface

Anything dead coming back to life hurts.

—Toni Morrison

WHEN I STARTED THINKING about writing this book, Toni Morrison's quote was the first thing that came to my mind. It was as if she was standing right behind me and speaking to me in gentle, hushed tones. Of course, it was only inside my head. The real Toni could not have come, she'd passed away recently. Well, even if she were alive, let's face it, it's unlikely that she would've come. The voice was actually my mother's, my Aai's, hiding behind Toni's face, because in imagination one can do that. Of course, something this sinister and beautiful had to come to me in the voice of my Aai. She, after all, is the source of all my wisdom, of all my anxieties, of all my maladies, and of all their cures. This book, said Toni-Aai, will be your awakening. The good daughter that I have always been, I wrote this down in my diary and said to myself, *this book will be your awakening.*

If I were to begin mapping my journey with illnesses, I would have to begin with a fateful night in January 2014, when I found myself riding an ambulance for the first time in my life. In those days I was still living in Delhi, in one of the new refugee colonies in what was known as Lal Dora land. Those were also the days when I was still happy. But I should have taken into account the fleeting nature of happiness. I should have known that all it really took was one bad second, and life as we know it, could change forever.

My body had been giving me warning signs for a week before that night. My stomach was making noises and I wasn't holding food in well, but I wasn't unduly worried. I kept thinking it would go away on its own, didn't it always?

Saturday arrived. After the pressures of the week, this was my time to unwind. We decided to order take-out and binge. It was a huge mistake. My stomach, which had valiantly held up until that point, couldn't take it anymore. My visits to the loo started somewhere around afternoon and did not stop for the next four days. I was severely dehydrated, but my body couldn't rest. At around three in the morning when my flat-mate and lover, let's call him Avinash, realised that it wasn't going to stop, he called the hospital.

The ambulance took all of 30 minutes to reach my house, the paramedics ran some basic tests—blood pressure and blood sugar—of which the pressure was low, the sugar normal. My apartment was on the third floor of a decrepit building that had no lifts. The paramedics asked me if I'd like to lie on the stretcher so they could carry me downstairs. Now, I do love dramatic entries and this could have been a shining moment of my life, but I declined politely. I am an overweight woman, you see. I didn't want the burden of my weight reflected on the faces of the men carrying me. I walked down the stairs, towards the ambulance on my own and got in, a wide grin on my face. Avi and I were beginning to find this entire episode funny. All we needed was a background score here, to indicate scatological humour, straight out of Bollywood. As it turned out, the joke was on me.

As soon as we reached Max Hospital, I was rushed to the emergency room where I lay on a bed waiting for the doctors to come and decide on my fate. When a doctor came to check on me and asked how many visits I had already paid to the loo, I smiled and told him the number had to be somewhere between thirty and forty. He looked troubled, but also vaguely impressed, though the latter could be pure fiction—the loss of fluids may have made me rather delusional. It was immediately ordained that I spend the next few days in the hospital. My blood was drawn for a CBC and a blood culture test and then I was wheeled away for an ultrasound. The results would take time, but in the meantime the doctors were drawing a recovery plan for me.

It was a long two hours before they informed me that I was probably suffering from an infection which was causing me all this trouble. They would give me some mild medication to control the frequency of loo visits and stop the stomach ache, but there was little else they could do. I would just have to ride it out and push the infection out of my body on my own. I spent the next four days in the hospital doing just that.

The next day my parents arrived in Delhi to be with me. So what if I had been hospitalised for just a stomach bug, a hospital stay warranted all kinds of attention. In the small provincial town of Jabalpur where I had grown up, I didn't have a lot of things that the big city kids did. What I did have was a dedicated set of parents, and over-involved neighbours who formed a safety net in my times of need. And this was a time of need. I knew what Aai was thinking when she made the decision to get on the train that would bring her to me. Who would spend all day and all night in the hospital with me? Surely I couldn't be left alone. Avi couldn't be expected to do it either, it would be too much of a burden. What if I needed something? What if the nurses abandoned me? What if they found out it was more than an infection? *What if.*

I hadn't realised it yet, but I wasn't very far from embracing all of Aai's anxieties.

Aai, in her usual manner, hugged me and cried a lot. The fact that her daughter wasn't dying or even sick enough to warrant an ICU admit, was completely lost on her. I told her not to cry. I told her I may not be fine, but I was getting there. I told her the mortality rates with my kind of condition, especially with my kind of privileges were very low. And she cried-laughed a little, and I felt the immense relief I had always felt around her. If she was here, I would be fine. If she was here, nothing would harm me.

As a child, on the rare occasion that I would take an afternoon nap, I would wrap myself completely in Aai's saree. Like a pupa inside a cocoon, I would be engulfed in her scent, her saree draped around my seven-year-old body. I would cover my eyes and drift off to sleep in its gentle, warm darkness. I used to sleep next to Aai till I turned six. Then my brother was born and I had to be moved to Aaji's room. But whenever I slept with her I would keep my hand on her stomach as I rested. Her warm, soft stomach, marred as it was with stretch marks, was the most comforting place for me. Perhaps a relationship I developed much before being born. Perhaps a metaphor for safety and comfort.

Now that Aai had arrived, I had the luxury of being violently ill. A panel of doctors walked into the hospital ward and greeted my parents. They then proceeded to inform us that what I had was indeed an infection. It was an attack of the Rotavirus. Until that point, I hadn't even heard of this particular virus and yet suddenly it had decided to set up home in my body. That year, I would spend a lot of time thinking long and hard about this viral attack and what it had meant for my body. Rotavirus, you see, is rather common, but it mostly affects infants, leaving the grownups quite alone. So why had I been chosen for this rare suffering, I wondered. It wasn't until much later that the answer came to me. How had I not seen it when it was always in plain sight?

The idea that I was being born again hadn't struck me yet. It would take a few therapists and several months of suffering to understand that this episode had opened a window to my past, where I was hiding secrets I was ashamed of. I would have to travel back in time and find that place where this pain lived. This pain that was hiding in my gut, rotting slowly, coming out in the form of stinky, disgusting bodily fluid had to be cured. It was time.

A few days after my parents' arrival, the doctors said it was all right for me to go home. The virus had left my body. I was healthy again. So far, though my body had been violently sick, the virus hadn't really scared me. In fact, I felt safe—I was in a hospital, surrounded by doctors and nurses, my parents were right at hand. Besides, I now knew I just had a diarrhoea producing virus. There was no cancer lurking anywhere; they would have caught it. My heart was healthy; they were taking my blood pressure every day and every day it was coming out clean. I was fine. I had to go home.

When I reached my tiny, and crowded at this point, 1 BHK—I was accompanied by both my parents, my brother, and my roommate—a cold fear seemed to be taking a hold of me. Suddenly, I was afraid. Outside the safety of the hospital, I felt I had little control over my body. This feeling constantly weighed on my mind. I kept refusing food. Something had changed. The hospital stay had ripped open some injuries I had completely forgotten about. When my body was getting rid of all of the unwanted fluids, I was, subconsciously maybe, also getting rid of a certain past that I had buried deep inside. My body was now empty, and I didn't quite understand this emptiness. It was sudden, I wasn't prepared for it. How do you fix something without knowing it is broken?

So instead, I focused on the tangible. I took my body, organ by organ, and tried to figure out what was wrong with it. I learnt how to count my heart beats. Why was my heart pounding at the rate of 95 beats per minute? Wasn't that high? The next minute it shot up to 120. Too high. I was sick. Why did my left leg hurt? Always my left leg. Only my left leg. Should I get it checked? Was peeing five times a day normal? Was my urine more yellow than it should have been? Why was I breathing like I needed to earn my share of clean air. Why was I stretching my lungs so much, every time I took a breath? Was it because I wasn't really using them fully before this day? Why was the pain in my stomach traveling to my back? Why was I nauseous? Maybe it was the sandwich I ate? But what if it was pancreatitis?

If I could, I would have washed each one of my organs. I would have rinsed them in the finest quality of detergent and hung them out to dry in the sun. But because I couldn't do that, I constantly thought about them. Soon the world around me ceased to matter. I only had time to think about myself. I only had time to figure out what each and every movement of my body signified. What was this strange chore I seemed to have signed up for without reading the documents?

That painful year is the reason I am writing this book. That is the year I lost my balance and fell off a cliff into a pit of gloom. That year I spiralled down the dark tunnel of ill health and injury. That year I discovered what lay hidden inside the deeper crevices of my mind. That year I opened my mouth and saw the universe. That year I interacted with the supernatural. That year my past and my present merged together. That was the year I was brought back from the dead. And if you aren't used to being alive, if your body has been lying static for years, any movement at all hurts like a thousand paper cuts. That was the year reality shifted from its axis. That year life made no sense. That year life finally began making sense.

I chose to begin this book from that year. Whether or not it makes narrative sense, this incident, and the clusters of memories around it, are why I am writing this book. In the pages that follow I will write about my childhood. And I will write about my adulthood. You will meet my Aai. You will meet my Aaji. I will show you my lovers. My new scars. My new-old diseases. And I will show you how I am not letting anything end badly. Everything my life holds will be transferred to the pages of this book. It's why I have to write this book. Because *this book will be my awakening.*

PART I

1

I shut my eyes and all the world drops dead;
I lift my lids and all is born again.
(I think I made you up inside my head.)

—Sylvia Plath

WHEN AVINASH AND I started falling in love, we had already known each other for two years. We had been there for each other's heartbreaks, for illnesses of parents, struggles with jobs, everything. Away from our small-town homes we had become each other's family much before we decided to be together.

The year we met was also when Delhi was getting ready to host the Commonwealth Games. The streets were crazy shiny and determinedly poverty free that year. We were in the same college studying journalism and we were neighbours. In the tree-lined streets of Greater Kailash II, where both of our paying guest rooms were situated, we became friends.

The thing about Avi was that he was easy to fall in love with. He'd crack a joke at the most inopportune moment, and despite yourself, you'd smile. He knew all the trashy Bollywood songs. He knew all the cool, lesser-known writers.

And he was always dripping with a brooding sadness, as if he had just walked out of a black and white French film. All these things, but most of all the sadness, made me gravitate towards him. He was one of those boys you'd want to take care of. Which is why he was popular in college. He was tailor-made for puppy love.

Avi and I both revelled in the idea of sadness. In those days, my PG-mate had a boyfriend she often whined about, who would be in our room almost all the time. Boys were allowed in our PG, which was quite unusual in Delhi at the time, but my roommate's good fortune was the bane of my existence. While she and her clingy boyfriend binged on *Modern Family* episodes, I hit the quiet streets of GK II. And Avi, because his room was way more chaotic than mine, joined me.

Our friendship was cemented during these endlessly long walks. We explored every single gully of that neighbourhood. One bungalow after another, we looked at the intimidating structures of Delhi's domestic life. We mocked their names, some of which reminded us of infamous Bollywood super villains. There was, for instance, a Balwant Rai who had a bungalow there, and quite like his evil namesake in the 90's hit *Ghayal*, he did have dogs.

We walked through the fashionable M Block market where the only affordable place for us was a 24Seven store that we frequented to buy Sour Punk, cola flavour. We had befriended an ice cream vendor who would be found in the same spot every night, listening to old Bollywood songs being played on all the late night radio stations. Avi and I would buy orange popsicles from him, ten rupees a pop, suck on them, and glide through the night discussing what all young people, who think they are the first to truly experience existential angst, discuss. He often talked about John Keats. How Keats could never be with the love of his life. How Keats died at twenty-seven without any recognition. How, much like Keats, he too might die young.

Avi was in love with another girl in those days. I am going to call her Kritika. He used to write poetry for her. And make me read it. I'd be awed.

'I almost wish we were butterflies and liv'd but three summer days—three such days with you I could fill with more delight than fifty common years could ever contain.'

He showed me this line one day, and said, 'Isn't this the most beautiful thing you have ever read?' It was, of course. 'I am so proud that I know someone who can write like this,' I said. He laughed.

'The words belong to Keats,' he said. 'I am borrowing them because this is how I feel about her.' And I looked at his face in doe-eyed wonder. Why was Kritika not falling in love with him? Wasn't he the perfect guy? Some women were so blind.

Love was something holy for the both of us. We were from the *Kuch Kuch Hota Hai* school of thought that believed in falling in love only once, though we never brought this film up as a reference point. It would have been too plebian for our tastes. While Avi had Kritika, I had my own drama playing in the background. I was in love with an old friend, (let's call him Aditya) who wasn't in love with me because he said, and I quote, 'I am not capable of love.'

Neither of our love wagons was making any progress, it did not matter though. Love wasn't something that could be forgotten. Requited or not, love was here to stay. Would it even be love if we ever got over it, we'd often say. Growing up, Eric Segal's *Love Story* was one of my favourite books. I had spent many a teary-eyed evening reading it. In Oliver's Story, the sequel of the book, we find that Oliver never really moves on from his wife's death. That sealed the definition of true love for me. Once you fall in love, there was no falling out of it.

By the end of that year, Avi and I had become close friends. College was almost over and it was time to give up the PG life. Because we enjoyed each other's company so much, we decided to live together. What could be better than living with a friend, right? By June 2011, Avi and I had left the posh lanes of GK II behind and rented a 2 BHK in an up-and-coming urban village. I soon started working with a magazine as their feature writer. He joined a newspaper. Our new lives had begun.

But the baggage of our former lives remained. Avi was still in love with Kritika. Meanwhile, I hadn't talked to Aditya in months and I wasn't missing him all that much. But one day, out of the blue, I got a rude, angry email from him, accusing me of things I hadn't done. And while I can now say with certainty that I was never in love with him, when the letter landed in my inbox, it left me shaken.

Later in that week, Avi and I were lounging about in my bed, talking about the letter that had upset me so much. It was a warm September night. We didn't have any ACs or coolers in our house, just one lonely fan and it wasn't enough to keep us comfortable.

It had been a bad week. I was restless and needed someone around me so I could fall asleep. As I was slowly drifting away, it happened. I remember it so well. I was lying on my back and he was on his side, facing me. I turned to my side, with my eyes closed—I was trying to sleep after all—and my lips brushed against his, and just stayed there. I don't know how Avi felt in that moment but I felt like someone had nailed me to the spot. I wanted to move but I could not. I kept wondering why he wasn't moving. *He should move. I should move.* In what felt like the longest moment of my life, I was stuck in a cramped room with my lips gently touching his. And then we kissed. An urgent, tender, passionate, bad kiss.

We decided to date. When we told friends, they rolled their eyes and said, 'It was bound to happen, what took you so long?' We had no answer.

Once we started dating, Avi and I began doing everything together. Most of our time that wasn't spent at work, was spent watching movies together. We loved listening to film songs, old and new, especially the 90s Bollywood music that we had grown up on. The Central Board of Film Certification (CBFC) had restored some of the Indian New Wave films from the '70s and '80s and Avi hadn't watched any. He

bought a DVD player and we started buying DVDs—Govind
Nihalani's *Party*, Gulzar's *Aandhi*, Sai Paranjpe's *Katha*, and
Raman Kumar's *Saath Saath*; we bought them all. The last
film was my choice. I insisted that he watch the film that
had come to define much of my understanding of love as a
child. I, like Deepti Naval, would have followed my morally
upright lover to the end of this world, I thought. What was
love without class conflict and misguided ideas of Socialism?

Our weekends would be spent trying to read books
together. But reading is a more solitary pursuit. Books aren't
movies, two people can't read from one book, not without
getting frisky. But we did try in earnest. We found a depressing
book—sadness the core of our relationship still—Michael
Ondaatje's *Divisadero*, and began reading it.

I read loudly from the book, and Avi listened as he ran his
fingers down my back. I'd say the small of my back, but my
back is anything but small. This line from the book would
later prove prophetic. But in that moment, oblivious to the
future, I read and I giggled.

We even bought a few poetry collections of the famous
Romantics together. Poe and Wordsworth, Keats and Byron,
were all our companions in love. Our library was growing. We
needed a place to keep our books. We went to the Munirka
furniture market and bought a small bookshelf, which would
later double as the TV stand, and brought it home.

On a Sunday when we were arranging our books Avi said,
'Look at our growing collection!' He sounded so proud. We
both were. I asked him what we'd do with the books if we

split up. Our divorce would mean splitting these books into equal halves. 'Impossible!' he exclaimed. 'Neither of us is parting ways with our books. We are never getting divorced.' We were in this for life.

We had big plans of seeing the world together. We would often check the flight fares, estimating the money we'd have to save to travel to all the remote countries we wanted to visit. We wanted to travel to all of Scandinavia, especially Iceland because it was the best country for writers. Iceland loved writers and we wanted to be beloved writers. We wanted to grow together, and become famous together. We wanted to surprise the world with our talent. Even if we couldn't do it in this lifetime, we'd do it posthumously, like Keats.

Avi was John Keats. And I was in constant awe of his demure nature. His silences were filled with pain, his kind eyes could only belong to a puppy. He was perennially mopey but in an endearing way. He suffered from a bad childhood. His parents loved him, perhaps a bit too much. His mother called him six times a day. She would refuse to eat food if he hadn't eaten. She would panic and call all his friends if he didn't take her call. She would not give him any space. And it made him angry. He and his mom fought a lot. They could fight over anything—why he hadn't eaten that day, why he had only eaten a particular thing another day, why he had refused to meet a relative, why he had met a friend who she didn't approve of. There was a lot of resentment and anger on both sides. He sometimes threw things at the wall in frustration. These outbursts scared me. It seemed to me that Avi was choking. He could not breathe on days. Love had become an asthmatic curse for him. So, naturally, he turned to me.

Avi's torrid relationship with his mother meant that he began emotionally depending on me quite a bit. I was beginning to become his world. I was at the heart of everything. And I would be lying if I said I didn't like it. I did. I loved the importance, loved the illusion of power I had over him. We were predestined for love and success, perhaps even fame—this was a sign. I would do everything to help him, even if it meant putting his needs before mine. He was opening up to me, he was breaking free from a shell, and that had to be hard, I told myself. So, even if I ever felt tired of the emotional labour I was doing for him, I wouldn't give up.

I reached a point where I had become so important in his life that I was redundant. Somewhere, somehow, we forgot that I, too, existed in this relationship. And when the realisation struck, neither of us was prepared for it.

Jeanette Winterson famously wrote of love in her book, my bible, *Why Be Happy When You Can Be Normal*. She called it a difficult word, where everything begins, where we always return.

When I jumped into this relationship it was with a hope of returning to love. When I made the leap, I realised how ready I was for it. I also realised how not-ready he was. But I kept telling myself it was not going to be a problem. Eventually we would align. I had no idea about what would happen next.

Avi had never been one to leave people behind. Once you were in his life, you were there forever. It didn't matter who you were and what relationship you shared with him. It was a quality I deeply admired. It was reassuring to think that I was here to stay, that our relationship was not going to have an end. But it also meant that Kritika would never be leaving either. Add to that the fact that, although he didn't say it out loud, I could see that he was still in love with her.

It was a constant battle with invisibility interspersed with moments of happiness. It wasn't all bad and I told myself it would get better. I would have to wait. The Barthean idea of love, after all, was that. A 'lover's fatal identity', he called it, was to always be the one who waits.

If it was good enough an idea for Barthes, it was good enough for me, right? Not quite though.

The thing with Avi was that he was the most sensitive and caring friend you could ask for. His presence in your life meant devotion. He couldn't bear to see his loved ones suffer. He would stay up all night talking if he sensed I was feeling lonely that day. But he was also quick to take advantage of my emotional availability.

A few months after we started dating, Kritika informed him of her engagement. News of an ex getting married not too long after a breakup always hurts, I suppose. But what is the right way of dealing with it? I still don't know the answer to that, but I do know that going to the engagement party and dragging your current girlfriend along is probably not the best way. But Avi insisted and I relented.

On the night of the engagement, we quietly got ready. It was an uncomfortable moment for the both of us. Avi knew

I didn't want to go, but he also knew that he had to go and he needed me. We took a metro to Punjabi Bagh and reached the venue after an hour and half of struggle. In an ornately decorated hall, Avi's ex-lover was getting engaged, and I could see the wind getting knocked out of him. I, meanwhile, was trying to figure out how I fit into this equation. I tried to ignore the knot of discomfort I felt in my stomach and tried to swallow the resentment I was feeling towards him. Oblivious to our dark mood, the bride-to-be dragged us to the dance floor. It was a classic Bollywood moment. She should have given Avi a mic to sing into instead. *Teri galiyon mein na rakhenge kadam*, Avi could have sung for Kritika, like Anil Dhawan sang for Neetu Singh.

'Do you want to eat something?' I asked him. He said no. 'You go ahead if you want to.' I told him I wasn't hungry even though I was. I asked him several times, if he wanted to leave. He refused and instead chose to walk around like a zombie. By the time we left the venue we had missed the last metro. And we were too broke for a cab. On a cold November night, we returned home in an auto. I remember shivering throughout the ride. When I got under my quilt, I was unsure if it was the hurt and anger making me shiver, or just the cold.

'I am really sorry,' he said. 'I shouldn't have gone there, I shouldn't have taken you.' I burst out crying. I calmed down in some time and quietly ate the Maggi he made. As humiliated as I was, I was also hungry.

This incident would return to me every time we fought over something, every time I swallowed my anger at him to avoid making a bad situation, worse. But I would quickly shove it aside instead of addressing it, because while sometimes it was bad, other times wasn't it great?

When Avi finally got over Kritika, almost seven months into our relationship, things changed. We became obnoxious lovers. We started leaving our marks behind everywhere we went. We indulged in serious public display of affection. We discussed it too. Would we like to kiss at the airport that was always crowded? Of course we would. I had gone home to Jabalpur for Diwali, when I returned to Delhi after a week, Avi came to pick me up at the airport. We kissed in front of the Arrivals Gate of the Indira Gandhi International Airport, Delhi, while people watched us. Some even made judgmental faces. But it was an important kiss. My inner small-town M wanted trademark big city moments, and this was that for me. Later on, picking each other up from the airport became our relationship ritual.

We had quite a few of these rituals, these 'relationship things' that we celebrated. I remember early in the relationship, I couldn't bring myself to fart in front of him. I would either hold it in, or rush out of the room. One day I couldn't do either. Sitting in the living room, in front of the television with Avi, I farted. He looked at me and I smiled like a kid caught mid-mischief. He let out a loud laugh. And I laughed along.

Later, he came up with an idea. If we were to live together, he said, we would be farting in front of each other too. 'What's there to be embarrassed about?' he asked. 'From now on, if

I fart in your company, you clap. And if you fart, I clap.' It was a terrific plan, really. We had to embrace whatever was ours, because we loved each other and that included our warts and our farts.

This was it, this was love, I'd often say to myself. Sun shining, birds chirping, trees swaying, the whole jazz. Wasn't this how love feels? We had cutesy nicknames for each other. We had our trademark love songs. We had created an alternate reality for each other where our other problems didn't exist, only ridiculous amounts of happiness. How long could that last?

Avi's parental issues continued. His mother's affection continued to smother him, seemingly more than before. The days they'd visit him were the hardest of all. Trapped inside the suffocating rituals of religion, tradition and superstition, his mother would make it impossible for him to function. It didn't help that he hadn't learnt to draw a line and distance himself from this, emotionally. So it kept affecting him. I often got the feeling that while he did love his mother, he didn't like her very much. Today, when I think about her, I understand that she, too, was trapped, but it was hard for Avi to see that because he was also the victim of the situation.

Sometimes when she'd visit, she would fight with her son in a language I did not understand, but I could understand the anger. I remember sitting in a corner watching them shout at each other. There was a lot of rage in that house when she visited.

I felt I was becoming a casualty of this undesirable situation. Something that had nothing to do with me was becoming my everyday problem. His relationship with her was changing his relationship with me. How she behaved with him determined how he'd be with me. The angrier he got with her, the more strongly he'd want to hold on to me.

There were days when I'd want to break free, when I'd not want to be there. But sometimes Avi treated our relationship as a contract. Hadn't we promised each other to be there on good days and bad? We had to live up to that promise on every bad day, or he'd never forgive me. How could I abandon him midway? Wasn't I his family now? His lover *and* his mother?

I was too afraid of hurting him. With every growing fight between us, with every banged door, with every bottle thrown at the wall in frustration, my fear grew, and so did his attachment to me. He repeatedly told me how much he loved me. How he could not live without me. How I was the best thing to have happened to him. He'd be lost without me. His love was beginning to suffocate me. He was doing to me what his mother had been doing to him all his life.

It has, after all, been the curse of humankind. Each one of us will eventually transform into a version of one of the parental figures in our life. Unless we fight it hard. Mostly it is our mothers, those figures of absolute devotion in early life. We may have made different choices in career, in love, but it all changes when it comes to our subconscious reaction to stress. Every day I realise how much I am like Aai. My reaction to stress is the magnified version of her reaction to stress. She can't keep calm, neither can I. Avi was no different.

There is research on this phenomenon and it has been written about extensively. According to some findings, the key to understanding our behaviour lies in studying neurosciences. Our brain is programmed to formulate patterns from our first day on this planet. Since our mother is the first being we form a relationship with, these patterns are formed inside us through the interactions we have with her. And this especially comes out when we are under stress. Our neurons wish to take the familiar pathways, which have remained imprinted in our minds through unconscious memory.

If, for example, we have seen our mother resort to violence under stress, we will have the urge to replicate that as a mode of release. Avi had seen his mother scream, cry, howl under such circumstances; he had seen her cling tightly to him, to his father. And that was his standard reaction too. Every fight with his mother meant an increasing show of love towards me. He was doing to me what he hated the most. The difference was, while he could escape his mother—she was in a different city, he could make excuses, hide from her and not engage—where could I go? I only had him.

One time his childhood friend visited while his parents were staying with us. I was grateful for his company during what was always a tense time. Whenever Avi would fight with his parents, his friend would sit with me cracking jokes. Sometimes he would even provide a commentary, explaining what the fight was about. This time, it appeared, they were fighting a lot about me. I seemed to be doing everything wrong, crossing his mom's religious and superstitious beliefs. I had sensed her displeasure in her passive aggressive behaviour with me, but with Avi she had all her war weapons out.

His friend left while his parents stayed. I was sorry to see him go. That evening Avi asked me if I'd like to step out of the house for a bit. I gladly agreed. I imagined it would be the two of us spending some time away from all the anger and fighting at home. I suggested Pema's, a restaurant we frequented in Malviya Nagar. I was hungry and looking forward to the meal. Avi, meanwhile, looked displeased. I wondered if it was me he was irritated with, maybe he couldn't fathom how I could think of eating when there was so much going on?

Once we reached the restaurant and I started fussing over the menu, his anger became more evident. 'I don't care what you order,' he said. 'Eat whatever you want to.' So I did. One plate of steamed paneer momos and manchow soup. As the food arrived, I asked him what the matter was with his mother and he listed out all the things I was doing wrong. 'Why can't you just wash your plates every time you use them till my mom is here?' he said. I felt attacked and retorted, 'Your mom rewashes the already washed utensils anyway. What a colossal waste of water when all of Delhi is thirsty.' It was an unnecessary social commentary, but still true. We were constantly running out of water and the building caretaker had complained about our water usage in the face of a major water crises. 'Don't I know that?' he snapped. 'You will just have to adjust till she is here. Then you can go back to being you.'

I was smarting under his unspoken insinuations, this had gone on for too long. 'Why do you guys keep fighting about me? I feel so worn out, so claustrophobic.' He didn't like that I was complaining. 'Here I am fighting for you every day and you are whining about it,' he said, incredulous. 'Can you not just adjust for a bit?'

I wanted to yell back. I wanted to say that I hadn't asked him to fight for me, I could handle things for myself. I wanted to say there shouldn't be any fights about me anyway, that it was unfair that I had to be subjected to this uncalled for anger. I wanted to tell him that he was a part of the problem. But I didn't. I kept it all inside my head, I fought all my battles there. I didn't want conflict. I told myself he wouldn't get it. And a lot of times, he did not get it. We paid for the food I had eaten, got an auto, and went back home, still angry and resentful, but quiet.

Without realising it, I was already leading a dual life. There was one in which I was Avi's girlfriend, where even when I was uncomfortable I was unable to confront him, because whenever I did confront him he somehow managed to make me feel responsible for the problem at hand. After repeating this pattern a few times, I was just afraid of bringing anything up. The other life was the one I lived inside my head, where I could say all that I wanted to, no holds barred. All my waking moments that weren't spent with him, were spent having these difficult conversations inside my head. There was just so much noise, so much chaos, that I felt like I was driving myself mad. The truth was I was lonely, the loneliest I had ever been, in the face of overwhelming love.

When I read my journals from those years, especially the later days, I often find short vignettes I used to write, that I would then turn into poetry. I absolutely detest the poetry I was writing then because of my humourless indulgence of my tragedies. The amount of self-pity embarrasses me now. I come across as someone who was not mindful of herself, someone who was quick to blame all her suffering on others. I wouldn't even acknowledge that I was broken, way before Avi came along. Facing my demons was hard, blaming him was so much easier.

Things did change and I did start seeing things with more clarity. But back then I was too hurt and too involved in my pain to see anything else. This is when I was beginning my journey as a writer. I started writing because, since I couldn't say things to Avi, writing about him seemed like the only alternative. 'I hate it when you write about me,' he'd say. And I would resent it. I couldn't stop writing. The easier solution was to stop showing him my poems. If I couldn't fight, and I couldn't write, where would that leave me? I would just accelerate the rate at which I was killing myself. I was, as it is, harming myself by making small cuts, pulling my hair, starving myself, and then overfeeding myself. So, despite his protests, I wrote.

When I cried sitting next to the water filter,
and you told me you loved me.
When I told you to not fix me,
and you did it nevertheless.
When our love broke my arms,
as we slept in each other's embrace,
and you still asked me to hold on to you.
Your dreams had turned against you,
and my reality against me.

2

'It's not true that life is one damn thing after another; it's one damn thing over and over.'

—Edna St. Vincent Millay

MOMENTS THAT CHANGE YOUR life are often unremarkable. One minute everything is fine—you are having dinner, you are watching television, you're walking in your carefully cultivated garden, and the next minute it has all gone wrong. People you love drop dead in front of your eyes and you are left wondering what you could've done differently. You step out of your house to meet a friend and someone runs you over. You lose a limb or two, puncture an organ maybe, and life as you know it has changed forever. Suddenly you become the tragedy that fuels conversations at family gatherings.

My life altering moment was terrible by all standards, but it didn't leave any visible scars. Hiding it was easy, so I kept quiet about it, even to myself. Instead of acknowledging it, I told myself I felt nothing. And for a while, I did feel nothing.

It took me nearly a quarter of a century and one epic stomach ache to realise that my life was falling apart. For me, the Rotavirus Attack of 2014 symbolised the opening of doors I had locked a long time ago to keep unwanted emotions away. For a whole week, I shat constantly, every few minutes. And while shit could just be shit, my shit, I know now, was a pain-in-the-ass metaphor for my mental ill-health.

It was a cold January morning. The small, ugly living room clock that Avi's parents had hung on the wall was smugly sitting at three. I had just come back from my zillionth visit to the toilet. I had not stopped pooping all day. I was crying. 'I want my Aai,' I said loudly to no one in particular. *Should I wake her up? Should I make that call? Aren't late night calls scary? What if they think I am dead? What if they don't take my call and I actually die of pooping. Do people die of pooping? Sure, poor people do, don't they?* Avi interjected my chain of thought and said, 'Just call them, tell them it's worse, they'll know what to do.'

I dialled the number. Baba answered the call, but before I could get a word out, he gave the phone to a panicked Aai. 'I cannot poop anymore, Aai,' I cried. 'It's hurting. It burns a lot, and it hurts, even though all I am passing is water.' Aai, on the other end of the phone had begun to melt into tears. 'Tila kae zala asel? (What must have happened to her?)' she turned to Baba for comfort. 'She needs to go to the hospital,' Baba said firmly to her, but more to himself. 'She should have done that in the afternoon. It's always the eleventh hour with her.' And then he asked me to put Avi on the phone. 'Call an ambulance and take her insurance papers with you. We'll be there as soon as we can,' he told him.

And that is how I found myself in the ambulance in the middle of the night. Avi started giggling, saying how he had never ridden in an ambulance. 'Thanks to you, I can cross off another experience from my list,' he said. I started laughing. The paramedic looked a little puzzled and a little irritated. He needed me to play my part of the patient well. I often remember the laughter we shared in the ambulance. That was the last time I laughed without the burden of fear and anxiety. I would have laughed a little longer, a little harder, had I known that my unremarkable, life-altering moment had finally caught up with me.

When I returned after spending a week in the hospital bed, an irrational fear accompanied me. Now that I was home and not in a place where I was being given round the clock care, I was afraid I might fall sick again. And what would I do then? I tried to reason with myself. Even if I fell ill again, unless it was something incurable, I would get better. Another stomach bug would not be my end. It wasn't the first time I had got a stomach infection and certainly wouldn't be the last time. I tried, but I couldn't get myself to stop obsessing about it.

'Constant diarrhoea, what does it mean?' I would type on Google search. No, I didn't get diarrhoea constantly, but I wanted to be prepared. 'Afraid of diarrhoea.' Another subject I searched. This one was to find a community of people who shared my fears. I discovered there were several support groups for diarrhoea sufferers. Look it up if you don't trust me. 'Symptoms of irritable bowel syndrome,' I typed. Because Avi said his mother had it. 'Can irritable bowel syndrome be cured?' Because he said his mom had been struggling with it for years.

One day, in my favourite tattered green Tantra t-shirt that flashed 'Lassi Jaisi Koi Nahi' across my breasts, I lay on the bed, curled up in a foetal position, holding my stomach and staring at the wall. My oily scalp, on several occasions, had left stains on it. An unsuspecting mosquito had been swatted to its death there, and I hadn't even wiped clean its blood. Or was it my blood? A notice board hung on that wall that had a never-changing to-do list.

My heart was racing, my hands tingling and yet numb, my skin burning, my tongue so heavy that forming words was impossible. I was living the nightmare that leads to sleep paralysis. *I cannot move. Will this ever be over?* I kept thinking. 'What is happening to me?' I asked Avi. He had no answer. 'It will be okay, you will be okay,' he said unconvincingly. *How does he know I will be okay?* I said to myself. *He doesn't know anything.*

By this stage, my fear had reached ridiculous heights. I had started relying on unnecessary medication. The slightest amount of gas in my stomach had me reaching for my medicine box. Pan D plus Aciloc, when taken together worked best for gas troubles. Only Pan D or only Aciloc wouldn't do the trick. O2 tablet was my best friend. That beautiful orange antibiotic tablet that could cure a variety of diseases from chronic bronchitis, pneumonia, tuberculosis, gonorrhoea, chlamydia, anthrax to even the plague, was my chosen drug. Any sign of pain or discomfort and I'd promptly pop one.

But most of the time there was nothing wrong with my stomach; my head, meanwhile, was a different story. O2 would stop my perfectly normal pooping cycle and make me constipated. My stomach therefore would still not be okay. But I'd refuse to give up the medication.

If you have ever watched a horror film, and if you, like me, are scared of ghosts, then you might be familiar with what happens when you go to bed alone after watching a horror film. After I watched Ram Gopal Varma's *Bhoot*, I started feeling like there was someone standing at the door of my room, staring at me. When I watched his film *Raat*, I made sure my bed was not resting against the wall anymore, lest two mouldy hands emerge from the walls to strangle me. Your overactive imagination makes you hear things. It's your mind playing tricks on you. But the fear is real and that tingling sensation you feel is your body reacting to this fear.

What was happening to me was no different. My life had become the night after the horror movie. Those hands coming out of the walls had grabbed me by the throat. My pain was standing at the door, constantly staring at me. My pain was my ghost. And I was feeling it in my body, even though it didn't exist. The formal term for that is psychosomatic pain. Even though it didn't exist, it was real for me, which meant I had to find a cure for it. So every stomach ache meant popping a Cylopam and sleeping in nervous anticipation of things getting worse.

I was perpetually in preparation for doomsday. The only difference was that my back-up supplies were medicines and only medicines. I was noticing every single sound my body made. I was noticing every single twitch. If my leg hurt, I immediately imagined bone cancer. My stomach ache which was so regular now, had to be stomach cancer. Even when Avi pointed out that this was just madness and that there was nothing really wrong with me, I would ask him, 'But what if there is something wrong? What will you do then?' Of course, there are no answers to 'what if'. And you cannot live in the fear of 'what if' either. But I was a prisoner of my mind and I could not escape.

I was so preoccupied with my imaginary diseases that Avi had slipped into second spot in my life. I had no time to think about anyone but myself. He was witnessing how I was falling apart piece by piece, but he did not understand what I was going through. How could he, when even I didn't?

Avi would often ask me to go for walks with him. 'We need to be healthy, M,' he'd say. 'We have a lovely park outside our house. Why not make use of it?' I would silently listen to him. I knew he was right. I even tried accompanying him a few times.

The jogging track of the park was a kilometre and a half long. There were days when we'd take three to four rounds before we headed back home. These were the magical days when things seemed possible. Other days would have me sitting on a bench while Avi completed his rounds.

One morning, as soon as Avi and I entered the park, I started feeling nauseous. I had heartburn and my stomach pain was back. Avi and I ran back to the house. Once we reached home, I immediately felt better. The nausea went away and the stomach pain disappeared. My body and my mind registered that as a sign. Any place other than my house and my bed was unsafe.

I stopped leaving my bed altogether. I was working from home back then, writing articles for a website, so I didn't need to leave the house all that much, or at all. My home was where the toilets were. I was to be found in my bed, all day and every day. Maybe I would die there.

January slipped into a warmer February. Soon it would be time to commemorate the first month anniversary of my descent into madness. I would celebrate it with yet another short hospital visit. After my first hospital stint, my relationship with food had deteriorated. I had, for the most part, given up eating spicy food or anything that I felt had the potential to carry infections. That entire year I did not eat any street food, much to Avi's chagrin.

'Why don't we walk to the PVR Saket market and look at Bhim uncle's stall to see if there are any new books?' Clearly, Avi knew me well. If anything could get me moving, this would be it. Bhim uncle had the best stock of second hand books in the market. PVR had a 24Seven store where we could get chocolates and some of the fancier things we liked to eat. But PVR also had a momo place we loved.

And a golgappa place that we loved. He'd try enticing me. 'Remember the time when we could eat golgappas? Wasn't that a great time?'

With all my heart I'd want to give in, but the fear was too strong. I was eating khichri on most days because it was light on the stomach. True, I was staying away from street food but it wasn't as if I was eating a healthy balanced diet. I wasn't striving to be healthy, I just didn't want to fall ill again. Come what may, I said to myself, I should never get another stomach upset. For someone who loves food as much as I do, this was tortuous. I knew it didn't make sense. But my anxiety won over my will and power to reason things out.

It wasn't as if this was the first time I had fallen ill. I had even been hospitalised in the past. I once had a urinary tract infection that went undiagnosed for the longest time. I remember being constantly unwell. I was in so much pain back then and my fever had spiked up to a little above 105 degrees.

After undergoing several kinds of blood tests—for jaundice, typhoid, malaria, tuberculosis—X-rays and ultrasound exams, and changing two doctors, I was finally asked to get a blood test done for UTI. I tested positive. By this point though, I had already suffered for a good two months.

With the new diagnosis came new medicines. I was to take twenty injections in the next ten days. Because I had been ill for so long, and been consuming all kinds of medication, my body had been stressed to the extremes. It rebelled and burst into excruciatingly painful haemorrhoids. A trip to the loo would leave me in tears for the rest of the day. I suffered terribly—I can't think of that time without a shudder—and yet it didn't scare me the way my diarrhoea had. Why?

The obvious answer could be that at the time of my UTI infection I was living with my parents. I felt safe in the secure surroundings of home and family. But the true answer was that I wasn't ready for fear then. I was ignorant. I maintained a façade of being whole. A medical emergency was just that and nothing more. My illness today is a metaphor for something so much deeper. Then it was just something I needed to overcome physically. Today, it was invading every aspect of my life—the physical and the metaphysical. Especially the metaphysical.

In the middle of a chaotic February came Avi's birthday. He loved celebrating his birthday. His otherwise grim perspective on life would be put aside for that one day. But there was no way we could have had a full blown party that year. Neither of us was a party person anyway. We decided to celebrate the day by going out. Which meant I had to make the effort of leaving the bed and dragging myself to a restaurant.

I was scared, but out of options. I could have refused to go and risked hurting his feelings, but after everything I was putting him through, I didn't have the heart to say no. By now I had settled into the habit of anticipating reactions, be it Avi's exasperation to all the crazy I was subjecting him to, or my body's rejection of practically anything. I felt so full of fear and worry, I had no capacity for happiness.

We picked a newly opened restaurant in Nehru Place called The Chatter House, invited a close friend, Navni, and called it a party. My plan was not to eat much, but the question remained: What would I eat? I picked up the menu.

Cheese tostadas sat at the very top of the list of starters. Rejected. It would have too many red chili flakes.

Rajma ki Galouti was next. No way, no kebabs.

Falafel with hummus, perhaps? Nope. Too much kabuli chana.

Jacket potato?

As I read the menu and rejected the dishes, Avi and Navni looked at me with amused expressions. 'Go for the jacket potatoes, M,' Avi suggested. 'Potatoes are light on the stomach.' I looked at him with suspicion. Was he lying to get me to eat? *Paranoid. You are paranoid*, said another voice in my head. 'That's what my mom eats when her stomach is upset,' he added when I didn't look convinced. I gave in, and ordered the jacket potatoes, hoping and praying that my stomach would accept the dish. I don't remember what the others ordered. I just remember sitting at the table, staring at them, slowing pushing jacket potatoes down my throat, as they devoured one course after another. It would be the first of many such half-hearted meals.

My original plan of not eating out at all had failed. I had kept it up for a month and a half after my attack, but soon realised it was not sustainable. There was take-out food that would be ordered because there was nothing to eat in the house on some days. There would be the occasional restaurant visits on dates. I knew we'd have to leave the house sometimes at least, but my fear and worry would overcome all reason. It walked with me every place I went. It sat beside me and stared at me, waiting for the right moment to strike.

I had many reasons to worry. Avi wouldn't have been able to take care of me the way my Aai and Baba could. I didn't want them to leave, but couldn't tell them that. I felt too silly to ask them to stay back because I, their grown up daughter, was afraid of a stomach bug. While they had been in Delhi, things hadn't been so bad. I was stepping out of the house with them—going to the neighbourhood park, the movies, taking a short walk to the vegetable market—but almost as soon as they left, my condition deteriorated. I was bound to my bed, and all of February, that is where I stayed. The only time I left the house was for Avi's birthday. February ended on that note.

We were now in the month of March. Hypochondria was blooming gloriously in my head. With nowhere to go, I was addictively watching one television series after another. *Grey's Anatomy*, *The Good Wife*, *Modern Family*, *The Big Bang Theory*, and whatever else was popular then was on my list. But *Grey's Anatomy* was the absolute favourite. I would watch reruns of it, sometimes to numb myself, sometimes to confirm the symptoms to my illnesses. It had just the right amount of medicine to feed my anxiety. It would scare me, and I thrived on that chaos. I could not explain it, even if I wanted to.

As Meredith Grey and Derek Shepherd's relationship was blossoming, mine was struggling. Where was the time to nurture a relationship with someone else when you were battling your own mind?

Sometime in the first half of March we left the house and went to watch the film *Queen*. We loved watching movies and dissecting them together. We'd often find ourselves catching the cheap early morning shows on weekends, an activity that had come to a crashing halt in this phase. I had starved myself the whole day and as an obvious consequence, in the middle of the film my stomach started making rebellious, rumbling sounds. It wanted me to feed it and it wasn't going to let me watch the film till I did, and so, in a fit of miraculous exasperation I went out and got myself a sandwich.

It was a plain cheese sandwich. It didn't have anything spicy, anything that could potentially trigger my stomach. Yet, the nagging voice inside my head kept repeating, *You are eating outside food? Are you out of your mind? This is how you will end up in the hospital. Stop eating. Don't buy it. Uff!*

As Kangana Ranaut's Queen drunk-danced to, 'Hungama ho gaya', a bomb exploded in my body. My stomach started hurting. I am still not sure if the pain was caused by the sandwich or my apprehension, all I knew was that it was there, and it was real. It was travelling to my back in strong waves every few seconds. It was a new variety of pain, like I had never experienced before, and it had me worried. I somehow sat through the entire film worrying throughout, trying my best not to panic.

During the interval, I ran to the loo. Shat. Didn't feel better. Opened my bag, popped two emergency Ridols that I always carried with me. Prevention is better than cure, right?

After the movie, Avi dragged me to the hospital. We were in the Select City Walk mall, only half a kilometre away from Max Hospital. After a full checkup, the doctor said, 'It's probably nothing more than a minor infection, but since the pain is travelling to your back, it could be a liver thing too.'

Panic began rising in my chest. I was asked to leave my blood sample at the lab, which would determine if I had another stupid infection or if my liver was failing. But who was I kidding? Of course my liver was failing. Immediately my brain got busy imagining all the plausible scenarios in case of liver failure.

Didn't Meredith give her father a piece of her liver in season 6? Maybe someone from my family would do that for me? Livers grow on their own, right? *And what about organ rejection*, said the voice in my head. *What if no one has a liver fit enough to donate? Have you thought of that?* As I was preparing to die while awaiting a matching liver, my reports came in. It was an infection. My liver would live to die another day.

Even though the report was clear, I wasn't convinced. I kept looking at it and checking each and every abbreviation. I googled and read up on every single thing mentioned in the test report. I had to understand what all of it meant. What if the doctor had overlooked something? It was tiring and so boring and yet my brain wouldn't relax.

It took a few days for my paranoia to pass. However, this hospital visit had an unexpected outcome—I stopped going to the hospital. The liver failure scare had shaken me up, and now I started associating Max Hospital with all the evil in the world. Once Avi was sick and had to go see a doctor somewhere. I hoped with all my heart that he wouldn't pick Max or at least that I wouldn't have to accompany him. But he did and I had to go with him. My stomach hurt all night that day.

All of 2014, I did not go to a hospital. All of that year I didn't face any serious stomach issues either. But that didn't stop me from stressing that my stomach was not doing well. I would keep popping medicines. My stomach maladies were like a bad song that I couldn't stop myself from humming. I hated it but had no choice.

Avi, Navni and all my other friends would keep telling me that it was all in my head. 'There is nothing wrong with you,' they'd say. 'You don't have any illness. If you keep looking at WebMD, it will say you have cancer. WebMD is not a realiable source, M. Don't do it'. Always the same line. 'It's all in your head. It's all in your head. It's all in your head, M.'

It might seem like I was caught in a saga of hopelessness, but of course, in between the difficult days there were the brilliant ones. The days when I could control my fears. When I could avoid thinking about all that was wrong with me. Those days Avi and I would be like the people we once were. We would be happy. We would do things we loved. We would watch a variety of songs on YouTube and sing along. We would spend nights sitting in front of one laptop instead of two. From S. D. Burman to Anu Malik to Amit Trivedi, all kinds of Bollywood music would be played, depending on the mood we were in. Sometimes it would be all the silly Govinda songs, on other occasions we favoured mushy romantic numbers. Then there were more sober days when we would talk all day and all night, without a pause.

Avi had a beautiful singing voice. It was a cross between S. P. Balasubrahmanyam and Hariharan but it was also very Avi. He was often out of tune, and almost always forgot the lyrics, but that never stopped him from singing. If he forgot the lyrics, he'd just make up new ones. This annoyed me endlessly and so, sometimes, he'd do it on purpose. And then I'd laugh, and he'd laugh. The house would reverberate with that laughter, so infectious, so precious, so easy to lose.

These moments would come often, but they were also fleeting. And neither of us chased them. The distance between us was growing branches. I was forgetting my older self more and more. I was discovering a new 'me' and losing who I used to be at the same time. Avi had been an integral part of who I was and in this process I was losing bits of him too.

I was angry all the time. I had never been great at confrontation. The relationship had begun with me taking care of him, and now, the responsibility I had unwittingly taken on was stifling me. I regretted it. I resented him for always being the fragile one. 'I have you and I don't have anyone else,' he'd say to me after every fight. And I'd feel more and more trapped.

Sometime in 2013, a year before I fell ill, Avi and I were working on a joint project that required us to travel to Maharashtra and interview people who spoke only in Marathi.

It was obvious that I would conduct the interviews since I spoke the language. We divided the work.

'I'll do the research, I am better at it,' he said. 'You frame the questions, do the interview, and transcribe it.'

When we had finished with the interviews and were back in Delhi, he asked me to write the story. 'I'll edit it and add my inputs once you are done,' he said. It seemed fair, I was the one who understood the entire thing in its language of origin. My experience in some ways was more immersive.

While working on the project, Avi and I started fighting over something trivial that I don't remember anymore. What I do remember is what he told me during the fight.

'Do you know why you are writing this essay and not me? It's because I care about your career.'

I was silent. Listening to him, trying to hold back my anger.

'I could have done a great job with this essay. But I want you to get better.'

I couldn't hold it in me any longer. 'Maybe you can write it yourself then,' I said. 'It's not too late.'

'That's not what I am saying, M,' said Avi.

'I am not your charity case. Don't treat me like one of your little projects.' I was regretting the words as they were leaving my mouth. But there was no taking them back. I was hurt. And he was being a total condescending jerk. I stood my ground.

But then he burst into tears. 'How could you say such awful things? Do you not know I love you? Am I not allowed to care for your career?' He fired one rhetorical question after another. He stormed off, banging the door on me.

There weren't many fights we had that reached their logical conclusion. Avi always walked out on me, wandered around, and came back like everything was normal. And I hardly ever got to say my piece. Avi, always the good guy, always the victim, always so fragile, so easily wounded you wouldn't want to touch him. And I did, I stopped touching him.

I swallowed and swallowed until I could not swallow anymore. Maybe this is why I was pooping so much. All this conflict brewing in my stomach had to find a release. Love, after all, was my sickness.

For the past one year I had been thinking about studying literature. I had always loved the idea of reading novels for education, but my school in Jabalpur did not offer Arts as a subject and I wasn't interested in doing my BA from the local university either. Now that I was in Delhi, now that I was already on my way to becoming a good enough writer, now that I was reading books that I wouldn't have even heard about had I stayed in Jabalpur, it felt like the right time to apply for MA programs and study. I wrote the entrance exam for Ambedkar University, Delhi, cleared the exam, and in no time I was a university student.

In many ways the university came into my life as a second lease. Education has always been a kind of savior for me. I would not have become a writer had it not been for a brilliant and ridiculously good-looking teacher in my journalism school. He was as critical of me, as he was appreciative, and he never stopped pushing me. With AUD it wasn't just the education—I had taken up a lot of interesting courses that really opened up my mind.

Another thing that happened in AUD was that I was introduced to therapy on the campus grounds. The university had come as a great distraction, among other things, but I was still just as paranoid and just as scared. The campus had an NGO called Ehsaas that offered therapy to students at throwaway prices and I jumped at the opportunity. It changed my life. I would never have found a solution to my non-existent stomachache, otherwise. I would not be writing this book, otherwise.

PART II

1

'Something magical has happened to me: like a dream when one feels frightened and creepy, and suddenly wakes up to the knowledge that no such terrors exist. I have wakened up.'

— Leo Tolstoy, *Anna Karenina*

I WAS BORN AND brought up in a small town called Jabalpur. I often have to explain to people, who look at me blankly at that name, that it is in Madhya Pradesh, that large central-Indian state no one cares about. It is perhaps why I feel tremendous joy whenever I find references to Jabalpur in pop culture, be it films, books or any trivia. My favourite of them all is from *Sholay*. The beedi factory where Sachin Pilgaonkar's Ahmed is headed, but doesn't ever reach because he is killed mid-way by Gabbar's henchmen, is in Jabalpur. Perhaps a great metaphor for the city that is so used to migration. You don't come to Jabalpur, you always leave.

Narmada, one of the longest rivers in India, flows through the city. Not far from my house are several of its banks. I have spent many a summer morning there. I learnt how to swim in the river because we didn't have many swimming pools in the city. And why swim in the chlorine treated waters of a pool when you have a free-flowing and largely clean, crocodile infested river to swim in? While most kids in my neighbourhood were fast asleep, my brother and I would wake up at 5.30 in the morning and leave for the river with Baba. One of Baba's friends was a swimming instructor who taught us for free.

The very essence of a small town existence lies in this concept of 'free'. I am not sure it's the right word even, because 'free' would indicate that there was a possibility of money being exchanged which had been foregone. In our case, it was a given that Baba's friend would take out precious time from his schedule to teach us swimming. Because weren't we like his children, too? Would he charge his kids? It is how life works in Jabalpur. Whenever anyone asks me about my city, the first thing I tell them is that it is a city of nice people. If you ever get stuck in the rain in front of a shop, the shop uncle or aunty will invite you in, make you sit, and give you chai. It's in a lot of ways like a big village, something I love and hate about it in equal parts.

The Jabalpur I grew up in was largely untouched by capitalism. We did have several important government-run factories there. The Indian army trucks are mostly all made there. I remember whenever we headed to the hills for our summer vacations, we'd often see army trucks and I would read the name of my city on them with unexplained pride. We had untouched beauty in Jabalpur. The crocodiles that ate half of Rekha's face in *Khoon Bhari Maang* were from Jabalpur. It's here that Hrithik Roshan fought the CGI crocodile in *Mohenjo Daro*. And it is here that Kareena Kapoor danced to 'Raat ka Nasha', in *Asoka*—in our favourite hang out spot, Bhedaghat, where we'd end up going every few days, and definitely every time we had guests visiting from outside the city.

Jabalpur was self-contained and good at keeping the rest of the world outside its limits. Life had a pace that was deliberately slow. No one was in a hurry to get anywhere. I grew up with that kind of leisurely pace, but I could never internalise the peace and tranquility that was its objective. I was an anxious child.

I was born into an upper caste, middle-class family that comprised my grandparents, my parents, and later, my younger brother. There was always some construction, some repair happening in the house in which I grew up. I'd often whine about it and my Baba would say it was not enough to build a house, you needed to keep redoing it. You had to maintain the house. Like life, you had to constantly keep making it better. While we strove to make it better, we were also very content. Our house that was always one room short to fit in all its occupants, had a living room big enough to fit in our middle-class aspirations, and that was enough to keep us happy.

I would roam around anxiously in that house every time my parents stepped out. Both of them had jobs and leaving the house in the morning was part of a routine I was used to.

It was when they had to go out to meet their friends, attend weddings or buy groceries that I would be worried. I would walk back and forth from my room to the living room, from the kitchen to their bedroom; I would map the whole house with my nervousness. Every time I would hear a scooter slowing down in front of the house I would run out to see who it was. Even though I already knew it wasn't them—I knew the sound of our scooter, their footsteps, their breathing so well—I liked to hope. I feared abandonment. Not that they'd ever leave me and start their own journeys. But what if they died in an accident? Or someone kidnapped them? There were always things to worry about.

I never shared that anxiety with anyone. I used to think it was normal to worry about your parents in this way—my parents who loved me so much and never gave me a single opportunity to complain. When other kids were acting out and cribbing about their parents not listening to them, I was smiling to myself, thanking the lord that I didn't have any such troubles. I had no need for childhood tantrums or teenage rebellions. I was born past all that. I was always a little surprised when other kids' parents didn't let them go for movies. Mine had always asked me to make my own decisions.

The first film I watched without them in the theatre was *Kaho Naa… Pyaar Hai*. I was in the seventh standard when the film came out. Some of my older colony friends were planning to go for it and asked me if I'd like to come along. I assumed I'd have to ask permission from my parents before agreeing to any such outing. I picked a time when they'd be too busy to think much about it. Baba and Aai were having breakfast, almost ready to leave for work when I popped the question at the dining table. All Baba said was, 'If you want to go, go. Just finish your homework. It's your decision.' It was something reiterated often. When our school took us on picnics, we'd be asked to bring permission slips. When I went to seek permission, I was told it was up to me. 'You write the note, we'll sign it.'

It won't be wrong to say that I was raised to think independently. In a conservative city where girls weren't allowed to stay out for long or play with boys, almost all my friends were boys, and most evenings I played late. There was a curfew of sorts, and usually I respected it, but on days I broke it and walked in late, Baba would announce, 'Rani Elizabeth padhar rahi hai.' Queen Elizabeth is here, finally. My Aai would frown at his lack of disciplining skills, but there weren't any punishments, not even enquiries. Baba's inability to scold anyone was a running joke between my brother and me. When, if ever, he got angry, all you needed to do was crack a smile and he'd start smiling with you, and just like that he wouldn't be angry anymore. Aai, on the other hand, took some time to calm down. She was a formidable force compared to Baba. But even she hardly ever lost her cool with us.

I realised even then that my parents were ahead of their times in the way they brought us up. No one ever shouted at us, let alone hit us. Parenting was a lot different in the

'80s and '90s and whacking your child into shape was quite common. Not in the Indurkar household. There was this one time, though. If you repeat this story in front of Aai, she will burst into tears. It's why I never bring it up.

It was a Sunday. I was about six or seven. I was sitting at the dining table, throwing a fuss about not wanting to drink my milk. I had thrown up after drinking milk a few days back and missed school. When I wrote that in my leave application, my teacher asked me to get checked for lactose intolerance. I wasn't lactose intolerant but I had discovered a new excuse to avoid drinking milk. And I planned to use it.

At the same time my grandfather was having a tantrum of his own. My otherwise calm and quiet grandfather was walking around expressing his displeasure at something by talking rather loudly to my mother. Which, in turn, gave my grandmother—who, like all Indian mothers-in-law, hardly ever missed a chance to find faults with my mother—a great opportunity to berate her.

It was all round chaos in the house that morning. So, when I looked at my mother, all smart-alecky, and told her there was no way she could torture me with milk, she flipped. Her intention was to push my chair away from hers. But she did it with such force that I fell off the chair, the chair fell on me, and broke. It was an old chair, anyway. Shocked at what she had caused to happen, my mother started crying. How could she hurt her daughter like that? To be fair, I wasn't hurt. And I wasn't sure why she was crying.

I acted all indignant and got a cloth to wipe the milk that

had landed up on the floor along with me. After that I went and sat in the living room, watching television. It seemed like the reasonable thing to do. That night, as a peace-making deal, I was treated to an ice cream soda with cherries. Oh, what a delight! I remember thinking it would be okay if I was thrown off chairs every day. This was a good bargain. But, much to my disappointment, that was the only time.

Growing up, I was never told that I couldn't do something. As far as my parents were concerned, I could have become a singer, a dancer, a painter, a musician, a karate expert, a basketball player, a mehendi designer, literally anything. Whatever classes I wanted to attend, if it was available in our small neighbourhood, it was made available to me. I wasn't the kid with the most expensive clothes or shoes, but I was the kid who went around doing all the extra-curricular activities she wanted, sometimes, all in a day. But I was also the kid who was easily bored. I took up Kathak, even appeared for the preliminary exam, passed it with distinction, and promptly gave it up saying it was encroaching upon my study time. And I was only in standard six, so you can imagine what a big fat lie that was.

I did pursue drawing and music for two years. But I realised it was mostly because my teacher adored me and I got great compliments in those classes. I enjoyed the attention. When that wore off, I switched to karate. I cleared the first two levels, and gave it up after becoming a yellow belt. I was quite directionless. But nobody enforced the idea of finding and sticking to a single thing that early in life. I got to try and reject everything. If I had had a different childhood, I wouldn't have discovered myself the way I did much later in life.

I remember I was in the third standard, all of eight years old, when my parents told me we were all going to Pune to meet my uncle and his wife. I had never heard of this uncle. My father told me he wasn't a blood relative. 'Just the son of your grandfather's close friend,' he said. My Baba's side of the family was like that. There were very few blood relatives. The people we were closest to were my grandfather's friends. Baba had grown up with their kids and they were all like his siblings. These relationships endure for him even today. It is no wonder my brother and I have such close-knit circles of friends. It's almost a legacy we carry.

The reason behind this sudden visit was that my uncle's wife had been diagnosed with a rare disease and no one thought she would be able to recover. This, of course, was the pre-internet era. Information wasn't as readily available. When they told us she had something called Myasthenia gravis, we were all worried. A neuromuscular disorder, it led to the weakening of her muscles. One moment you would be talking to her, another moment she'd have fainted. She was that weak. The access to proper treatment was proving difficult in India. The doctors had asked my uncle to go to the States for her treatment. My lower middle-class uncle obviously didn't think it was possible for him to do that, but since my aunt's condition was progressively getting worse, something had to be done.

During the visit I met their daughter. She was a quiet and intelligent girl. For years we'd keep hearing stories about her achievements. Her mother's illness had clearly had a deep impact on her. She told me she wanted to be a doctor when she grew up, but not just any doctor. She would be a scientist and a doctor, and like Smita Patil in *Dard Ka Rishta* working on a cure for cancer, she would be the one to cure Myasthenia gravis.

I, with all the sincerity and resolve my eight-year-old self could muster, told her I would be with her, every step of the way. In fact, I too would become a doctor and help her find a cure. I decided I also wanted to cure cataract because my grandmother had just undergone a surgery and she would often complain of itchy eyes and the fact that she couldn't eat eggplants that she loved because they made her eyes itch more. It was settled. We would be doctors, saviours of the world.

Apparently, at that point of time, there were only three registered cases of the disorder in the country, or so we were told. Luckily for my uncle, I suppose, Amitabh Bachchan was one of the three people. It excited me no end that I knew somebody who shared something so vital with Bachchan. What was even cooler was the fact that my aunt's doctor put them in touch with Bachchan's doctor and my uncle got to meet him. Bachchan ended up helping my uncle financially, and lived up to his saviour-of-the-poor-and-the-needy image, perhaps for the last time.

I was touched by Bachchan's gesture. My resolve to become a doctor strengthened. Can you imagine the fame I would receive if I cured Amitabh freaking Bachchan? I was excited. I started telling everyone back home that I would soon be a doctor. They all happily believed me. Why wouldn't they? The colony uncles would come to me and say they'd work as a compounder in my clinic once they retired. I would assure them jobs and promise them good salaries. It was a happy bubble.

In all this daydreaming, I had overlooked one tiny bit of information—I didn't have the smarts to become a doctor. The day I figured that out, I abandoned my dream. But, I'll have you know, my cousin did become a doctor.

While I eventually gave up on my dreams of fame and glory by finding the cure for a yet untreatable malady, I did use it for something else. I wrote my first personal essay for a school project. The topic was 'My Dreams' and it was about becoming a doctor. I used a fair bit of imagination in writing about a meeting with Amitabh Bachchan, and discussing his illness. It ended with me finding the cure to his ailment. My fourth standard class teacher was highly impressed. Not only did I know the name of a serious sounding disease, I had used that as a plug to present my dream.

My parents were informed about the essay and they were proud of their daughter's achievement. There was congratulatory joy all around, which, now when I think about it, was brought into our lives through a disease and someone else's misery. Over the course of the next several years I spent in school, I would write many essays including the one that would win me my first and only gold medal. However, these were all of a more socio-political nature—terrorism, environment, dowry, education of the girl child. I didn't write a single personal essay after that one.

The next one I wrote was in journalism school, and yet again, another disease was at the centre of it. I wrote about Baba's cousin, my aunt, who had died of cancer. I scored a spectacular A in the paper, but, more importantly, that essay rekindled the joy of writing in me.

It is funny that as an eight year old I started my writing journey with a disease that I hoped would shape my life. While nothing went according to that plan, diseases continue to be a preoccupation. Would I be writing this book had I not been a hypochondriac? Would I still be this person who I have come to like, had it not been for my obsession with diseases?

I have often looked into my childhood with hopes of finding clues to my dysfunctional behavior. It is hard to pinpoint when this obsession with diseases started and when I started sliding straight into the arms of depression. It has taken me close to two decades to even start this conversation with myself.

My entire childhood, in fact, could be defined as a period of self-imposed amnesia. I had so much to remember that I chose to forget everything. I locked things up in a corner of my mind and went about living my life. But that's the problem with hiding things from yourself, they always manage to resurface, in uglier forms. After two decades of keeping things hidden, when I finally allowed myself to look into my past, all I found were broken, incoherent memories.

Amnesia

Francisco walks, sleeps, eats and wakes up, some days in the same order. The broth of memory is placed clumsily on his side table. He consumes it a little, each day. He remembers some and forgets others. He calls Edna's name like he is calling Mary's. Who is Mary, he asks, why was she sitting next to me last night? She rocked that chair the whole night and made a lot of noise. She wasn't wearing clothes; she said she came in a hurry. Restlessly she tried to hold Francisco's hand but couldn't touch him. Mary wept like rain. When her tears couldn't touch the ground, she got angry. She cursed Edna and cursed Francisco. She stole Edna's clothes, wore them and left. Something broke somewhere; Francisco heard it and called for Edna. Or was it Mary?

This first poem I ever wrote—inspired as I was by Latin American literature then—was about forgetting. You probably won't find anything about my life in it. It's not even a good poem. But it is significant for it marks a new phase of life for me. In Latin American tragedies, I had managed to find my own. But the 'amnesia' was my doing. My past, like Mary from the poem, had started revisiting me. Mary would come to define an entire phase of my literary journey. But she deserves more than a tiny paragraph, so I will revisit her at another time.

Before I decided to stop weaving this web of lies around me, I would go around feeling smug about my perfect childhood. My perfect parents, my lovely friends, how loved I was even by the extended family; everything was right in my life.

My private life, though, was always at odds with this image I carried with myself. At school, I was at best an invisible child. At home I talked a lot, but got anxiety attacks the minute I tried to go to sleep. I didn't know these were anxiety attacks so I didn't know to address them.

I remember a Diwali night in particular when I was eleven or twelve and getting ready for the evening festivities. I had a new lehenga in a pretty peach that I had gotten stitched especially for the night. A big bag of fire crackers was waiting to be opened. My new jewellery, bought with so much care, matched my lehenga. Everything was right, except I couldn't bring myself to look into the mirror. I kept fighting an uncontrollable urge to cry. When I finally wore my clothes and jewellery and looked into the mirror, I immediately regretted it. It confirmed my fears—I was ugly. I couldn't step out of the house looking like that. I began crying.

My perfectly planned Diwali night was being ruined for some reason. I just didn't know how to save it. I told Aai, hoping she could help. She advised me to go out and be with my friends. I went with my share of firecrackers and stood there, watching everyone have a good time, while I sulked in my corner.

After an hour I came back because I wasn't feeling any better. If possible I was feeling worse. I went to my room and took out my science book. If I pretended to study, no one would say anything to me. I stayed in my room, silently crying into my book.

With puffy eyes, I looked into the mirror again. Someone

even uglier looked back. What had I expected? I was ugly, after all. Fat and ugly. Ugly and fat. This was the first time I thought of myself in these terms. But things were about to get so much worse. Or maybe, things had already worsened and I was just in denial.

That was also the year I felt the first wave of my health anxiety. I learnt about HIV and AIDS through one of the government sponsored commercials that used to be played in theatres. Shortly after, I fell ill. I convinced myself I was HIV positive and about to die. Any day now, it would happen. I worried incessantly about how I would convey this to my parents. AIDS had no cure, no medication, nothing in those days. It was also a disease you had to be ashamed of. What was I going to do?

I had thought I'd be taking my secrets to my grave. My disease, though, would show my true face to the world. And I wasn't ready.

2

'Surgeons must be very careful
When they take the knife!
Underneath their fine incisions
Stirs the Culprit—Life!'

—Emily Dickinson

Growing

Aai once told me if I swallowed seeds of fruits, a tree might grow inside me. And its branches might come out of my nose and my mouth. I always wondered how seeds could survive the hostile environment of my stomach. My stomach isn't like Aai's. It doesn't have the tenderness and adaptability of motherhood. If I could become a tree though, I'd be an orange tree.

All my fruit memories are salty. A friend, who I was once close to, taught me the difference between a kinnow and an orange. And I feigned understanding. She carefully cut the kinnow, sprinkled some salt over the slices, took out two forks and handed me an expensive china plate that her mother had brought from Japan. When I returned home I began craving the china and the fork.

When my desires couldn't be met, I ate an orange, misplacing its identity, perhaps forever.

In days of summer holidays and childish bets, I was asked to eat a spoonful of salt. The future of a hoard of green guavas depended on my salt absorption abilities. I ate that salt, won those guavas, and lost my childhood to them. After that day, I ate everything with a pinch of salt. I take that back. Since that day, I have been eating everything with a pinch of extra salt.

If a tree could grow inside me, I know it would be a guava tree. Even though I wouldn't want to smell like a guava, it's what would happen because of the seeds I have swallowed. It's hard to spit out guava seeds. I would say the same thing about strawberries. But strawberries are part of small town aspirations. They would be served on expensive china bought in Japan. When Aai bought guavas she chose the green, hard ones for me. On a steel plate she would put a spoonful of salt, and unknowingly ascribe a taste and smell to my tragedies, and expect me to thank her for the trouble. It's not easy to slice hard green guavas. I know.

Small towns, that are suddenly so popular in our cinematic universe—as if before this we didn't exist—have some very typical qualities. When I say that the colony I lived in was a big, annoying, messy family, I am not being hyperbolic. It was as oppressive a space as it was generous. Growing up in the late '80s and all throughout the '90s, we didn't have many things. At least individual families didn't, but as a group, we had everything.

My house, for instance, was the first to get a telephone

in the neighbourhood. So, most of the colony passed on our number to their relatives and friends. We would receive calls for various people and I would then go running to the house of the person whose call it was. 'Drop whatever you are doing and come,' I'd say, 'they're going to call back in ten.' The concept of waiting on a call didn't exist of course. No one was that rich. I remember the first time we got an international call. Because I was eager to talk to someone on the other side of the Atlantic, I was taught the proper protocol. I was supposed to say hello, then wait for a couple of seconds for my hello to reach them. And theirs to reach me. It was a thrill never to be replicated.

We didn't have a coloured television, but our neighbours did. So, it was obvious that our Sunday mornings were spent in their house watching *Ramayana* and *Mahabharata*. On some days there would be a post-lunch movie session on a rented VCR. Other times, we'd get a dinner invite to watch whatever film Doordarshan was telecasting that weekend. Two such distinct memories are of the films *Surakshaa* and *Phir Teri Kahani Yaad Aayee*. *Surakshaa*, not to be confused with the Mithun Chakraborty starrer *Suraksha* with a single 'a', was watched on the VCR. Initially it was supposed to be us kids only but then the parents decided to join in, as they often did. Everyone cooked something and brought it along and we all ate sitting in front of the television, watching what was a really terrible film. *Phir Teri Kahani...* was a more elaborate affair. Our neighbours decided to invite us for dinner the day the movie was to be aired. I remember the exact meal that was prepared—a very spicy anda curry, daal, roti and jeera rice. There was also the winter staple, gajar ka hawla, to be polished off post meal to balance the spiciness of the curry.

I was still very young and not used to staying up late in the night. Besides the film's storyline of a recovering alcoholic and a paranoid schizophrenic falling in love and singing sad yet lovely songs wasn't all that appealing. I fell asleep. Nobody woke me up or carried me back home. The idea of home was more fluid back then and so I stayed there for the night.

Another bizarre memory I have from that time was when I was obsessed with the idea of bathing under a shower. We knew a neighbour who had a shower installed in their bathroom. One morning I decided I had had enough, my urge to bathe under a waterfall emerging from a showerhead, had to be met. I told Aai I was going to the neighbour's to take a shower, took my towel and clothes, and left like it was the most normal thing to do. And it was. When I reached their place, they weren't surprised to see me either. Perhaps a little amused, but that was all. Their shower, after all, was my shower too.

The things I could do then aren't things I can do now. Though it still wouldn't matter much to my neighbours if I dropped by their place for an unannounced dinner or sleepover, because this ease and openness is stitched into the very fabric of this town. But I have changed. My anxieties have taken different shapes and forms and don't let me interact with people the way I once did. Even today, though, whenever any of my neighbours cooks something I like, it is sent over. Even if I maintain my distance, I am always remembered. It is something I am grateful for.

Growing up the way I did filled me with a sense of belonging. It taught me that no matter what, I would always have a place in the world that was mine, a place where my roots lay. It kept me grounded and assured me that even if I, at times, felt shelter less in the world, it would be temporary. I would always have a place to return to. It is this feeling that has kept me going, for despite all the bad things that happened to me here, there was also a lot of good. Enough good to keep my love for home alive.

Imagine a sleepy little town, a step removed from morbid consumerism, the shininess and cosmopolitanism of the metropolis and most things evil. Can you see it? Now imagine a colony, a close-knit community of people living in a peaceful neighbourhood. An unkempt garden with a big neem tree, two jujube trees, and that lush guava tree I want to talk about. It's a winter afternoon in December. The sun is shining brightly on a group of children lazing around on a jute mat. They are playing something, could be chidiya udd, could be cards. Could be antakshari. There is carefree joy on their faces. Can you see their faces?

'Who wants guavas?' says the man entering the scene and everyone is suddenly looking at him. 'Me, me, me!' I shout. But wait, let's name the man first, he is one of the reasons

I am writing this book after all. I'll call him Ajit, after the Bollywood baddie of the '60s. He is, if you couldn't tell, one of the villains of this story.

'You can't get the precious guavas that easily,' says Ajit. 'You have to do something for it. You have to eat a spoonful of salt. A big, no, giant heap of salt.' I am a cool kid. I live for such bets. I can do anything, what is a spoonful of salt? I accept the challenge. He brings out the salt container, dips a big spoon in it and extracts a mountain of salt. I close my eyes and dump the whole thing in my mouth quickly. There. I have won the challenge to a big applause. The guavas are mine to claim.

But winning the guavas isn't enough; I also have to pluck them. It involves climbing the tree and reaching the guavas. After eating that much salt, this is no big deal at all. Ajit says he'll help me in the task. I am still tiny, can't reach most places. I climb the tree and start choosing the guavas I will be eating today. The hard, green ones, I love those. He climbs the tree too and stands right behind me. I feel something now. Something poking me hard. He is busy plucking the guavas. What is it that is poking me? Why is he rubbing himself against me? Where did my guavas go? They have fallen from my hands. Cut. Cut. Cut. Everything goes dark. The memory ends here.

Bessel van der Kolk warns us in his book, *The Body Keeps The Score* that it is difficult to give your traumatic experiences a coherent order, a beginning, middle, and end. Which is to say, I do not know how to make narrative sense of my life. I began this book with the grown up M because it was important to establish that I have lived a life outside of trauma. That I have experienced love, joy, heartbreak. I haven't let my traumas completely dictate the terms of my life. Also, I can't claim to know for sure if this is how my journey with trauma began. It happened, but I cannot say with certainty if this was the first time it happened. But this is how I am choosing to begin my story. With the green, lush, juicy, fragrant guavas. My favourite fruit of childhood.

If you remember the characters that the Bollywood Ajit played, he was always the well-dressed, well-educated, rich, suave, evil mastermind. He lived in bungalows and had a Mona darling or a Silly Lilly as his decorative woman, always by his side. He was subtly funny too. The Ajit of my life was no different. He was smart, intelligent and possibly the funniest guy I knew as a kid. And I was, for all intent and purposes, his Mona darling. I was always by his side. He cracked the funniest jokes a six year old could understand. And I did like him.

He was a brilliant student, studying to become an engineer. As if that wasn't enough, he was polite, calm and helpful. And good looking too. Everyone's dream child; the one who made middle-class parents turn envious. They all wanted a son like Ajit, the villain of my story.

Whenever we played cricket, he would let me bat. Whenever we played hide and seek, he would find me, lift me from my hiding place and take me to his room. And undress me.

Nothing that happened to me was overtly violent. The

violence I faced was silent, almost invisible. I wasn't beaten,
I wasn't even yelled at. I surrendered to this abuse because I
didn't know any better. Six-year-olds aren't supposed to. Even
though it hurt a lot, there was some pleasure to be derived
from these episodes, and while my body didn't know much
else, it did know pleasure. I knew what was happening was
wrong, but I was also giving in to it. There were days I was
running away. There were days I wasn't running away fast
enough. And that gave way to guilt. So much of it, I feel its
burden even today, as I type these words, wondering what
you, my readers, will make of me.

Ajit wasn't the only one. There is a second villain in this
story. I'll call him Mogambo for reasons that are personal,
but also because he is the bigger, more heinous villain. The
one who caused the most damage. The one who infiltrated
my mind and never left. Quite like Mogambo, the cinematic
baddie who contaminated the country with kankad wali daal
and unsuccessfully attempted destroying the nation.

My experiences with these villains did, to use a tired phrase,
cause the death of my childhood. Though not completely. The
fact that I was in denial most of the time helped me escape
a lot of immediate damage these events could have caused.
I didn't understand what was happening, but that did not
mean I didn't feel its intensity. Or the guilt, shame, fear and
confusion attached to it.

I was made to taste his penis. Made to swallow his semen.
I was suffering every day, without really knowing it. There
are horrors in my past I wouldn't wish on my enemies. Like

the time when the beloved childhood VCR was brought out to play a porn film in my presence and I was asked to act like the actress in the film. Except, can six-year-olds do what those actors can? I don't remember the film. But the memory of that afternoon sticks to me like the remains of his assault on my naked body. That day he asked me if I'd come back to him when I was a grown up, and I promised him I would.

False promises that I never intended to keep because I never liked it when he touched me, it hurt a lot, it made me feel dirty, he scared me. Also because you see, I was in love with Ajit. To my mind, what Ajit and I had was special. We were in love and would marry each other, I assumed. Just like lovers did in the movies. When he wasn't sexually exploiting me, he was just very nice to me. We would crack jokes together, he would tell me about the world of books, teach me the value of a good education and make me believe that I was meant for bigger and better things. I loved everything about him and thought him perfect. Most people I knew agreed with me.

I wasn't emotionally equipped to handle all that I was feeling. I was too young to fall in love. Besides, there was no one I could talk to about it. Friends my age were not interested in such things. It was too removed from our world of childhood. It was more an idea borrowed from Bollywood movies. And it kept getting stronger with every film I watched. I was Madhuri Dixit's Nisha when I watched *Hum Aapke Hain Koun!* I was Kajol's Simran when I watched *Dilwale Dulhania Le Jayenge*. As an adult I have often thought about how patriarchy impacts our tiny minds. Growing up, I was an ambitious child. I wanted to be a doctor and cure cancer. But in all my love fantasies, I was a religious, mandir-going, married girl. I cooked and kept house for Ajit, the husband of my fantasies, and his family. Everyone in this charmed fantasy loved me, and why wouldn't they? I ruled the household and raised children. I was the perfect bahu of Barjatya's Bollywood. And oh yeah, I was also thin.

In a school fancy dress competition, I wore my red lehenga and dressed as a bride. I looked cute. I have several pictures. In one I am sitting in front of a mirror looking demure. During the competition, we had to go on stage and announce what we were dressed as. I went and spoke into the microphone. 'Dulhan,' I said, and since I was playing the shy bride, I did what I knew shy brides did. I pulled the ghunghat lower and swung lightly from left to right, right to left, and ran off the stage, making everyone laugh. I didn't win the contest. A girl dressed as a fairy did. She had a magic wand with a star on it and she used it to cast a spell. It worked and she won. In retrospect, I am grateful that childhood magic won over my child bride.

One day, while playing a game of hide-and-seek, Ajit lifted me from my place of hiding and brought me to his room. I was wearing a red t-shirt and a pair of denim shorts. He pulled them down and made me lie flat on his bed. The doors were closed. And then they weren't. My childhood best friend walked in, and Ajit ran away to the bathroom and locked himself in. She was the seeker and had been looking for me. Only, she had found me where she wasn't supposed to. I was angry and embarrassed. Did she really have to be this good at this game? She, meanwhile, was full of questions. It caught me off guard. I wasn't prepared for the possibility of having a conversation about this with anyone.

This is where my memory gets tricky. I remember the conversation that followed in two ways. And I am equally convinced that both the things happened, which makes me believe that there is a possibility that neither of the two happened. But let's play it scene by scene.

Scene 1: My BFF and I are sitting in the front yard of her house, talking. What was happening, she asks, and I tell her. Does it hurt, she says. I nod, it does hurt. How many times? Is it only Ajit? I say no. I tell her about Mogambo. I tell her he is the worst. It hurts the most when he does it. He doesn't care about me. But Ajit does. She nods like she understands the situation. Maybe she does. But she also looks sad. She feels left out. No one is including her in these games. Isn't she worthy of love?

Scene 2: My BFF and I are sitting in the front yard of her house, talking. So, it is happening to you too, she asks. And I nod, feeling angry, because suddenly I am not the only recipient of Ajit's love. But she says Ajit has never done it to her and I feel relieved. I am still the only one. It's Ajit's brother, she says. When he does it, it doesn't hurt at all. He doesn't even remove clothes, his or hers. He doesn't, I concur. It doesn't hurt at all. So Ajit's brother does it to the both of us. We look solemn and confused. What does this mean? No one has any answers.

The second memory came to me recently. And I remember

her voice, the confusion and sadness in it clearly, like it happened yesterday. It fills me with dread. Did the things that happened to me, also happen to her? Why did we never discuss it after that? Did we discuss it? Did she try to talk to me and I wasn't available? I know I didn't talk to her after this. I was ashamed. I was guilty. I was a bad girl. Could I have saved my best friend if I hadn't been selfish, caught up in make-believe love? The little girl in me feels the weight of this memory and stoops a little lower. But what do I do now? Do I talk to my friend? Do I bother her with this memory that maybe, didn't happen at all? What if she has forgotten about it? Do I have the right to bring those memories back? Do I need to injure her again? I don't have the courage to answer these questions.

Maybe, she will remain free of this pain and forever be in my mind the strange, carefree girl, who wore frocks with pockets on them. Pockets that were filled with snacks she liked. The girl I wrote about in an essay on my best friend for my fourth standard Moral Science homework. I got extra credit for pasting a photograph of her along with the essay. I still have that photograph. I still remember that girl, but the memory is somewhat tainted now. What I'd give to change that.

When I started working on this chapter, I dug up old photographs in the hope of them refreshing my memories. I am not sure it helped. Photographs, after all, are taken of moments one wants to recall. They aren't a document of history. They don't record your battles. They just catalogue your winning moments—your first step; the first time you opened your mouth and uttered your first words. 'Aai' was my first word—it couldn't have been anything else.

I have a picture from when I was probably seven years old. I am wearing a red t-shirt and black jeans. My hair is shoulder length and the straightest it has ever been. I am sitting in the middle of our small garden, in between two earthen pots, where two different kinds of roses are blooming. This picture, most definitely, is Aai's idea. I have a smug but happy expression on my face. I look at that picture and wonder if I was happy. I was happy. I most definitely was.

In another picture I am wearing a dark brown floral printed frock that my mother got stitched. 'Everyone loved your childhood clothes,' she tells me often. 'I bought the best cotton fabric and got it stitched from Amma.' Amma is her childhood tailor. 'Amma loved me and so she loved you, which is why your clothes were stitched with love. And they were the best.' This frock is no different. This frock is also love.

I am younger than seven in this picture. Maybe six. I have short 'boy-cut' hair. I am wearing a hairband and I am looking cute. I was a cute child, did I mention? Now that I am not cute anymore, the loss of my childhood cuteness is often lamented. I was beautiful and fair with pink cheeks. I was popular. Everyone said I could be a Cerelac baby. I am also wearing a big bindi that belongs to my Aai, in the picture. I look like a miniature Aai in this picture. I have always looked exactly like her. She is quite proud of the fact. Quite honestly, looking like Aai is only a privilege. There is no one prettier.

In the photo, I am eating. My mouth looks swollen because of the big bite of yet-to-be-chewed roti in my mouth and another bite, ready to go in, in my hand. There is no reason why this photograph even exists, but it does. As the first-born child of doting parents, my life has been well documented. And in every single photograph, I look happy.

For the most part, I was happy. But photographs don't capture the whole picture, do they? They are deceptive. As Susan Sontag wrote in her essay collection, *On Photography*, 'Life is not about significant details, illuminated in a flash, fixed forever. Photographs are.' I am glad these photographs exist and in such large numbers. Every small moment—that time I stood underneath a hand pump, soaking in the cold water pouring out of it, looking as happy as a one-year-old can; that time when I stood underneath a tree blooming with wild flowers, my lips red after chewing too much sweetened paan, with a few of those flowers neatly clipped on to my hair; all the holidays that I can remember and the ones I can't—they all exist in these photographs.

I have pictures where I look angry and sad too. In one of them I am crying, while my little brother is looking adorable, crawling right next to me. Then there is this one picture. Wearing a blue frock, sitting next to my grandmother, with some distance between us, I look haunted. And I can't help but wonder, did I somehow know then, that this picture would become a metaphor for our relationship? Had she already failed me by the time this photograph was clicked?

My grandmother, you see, saw Ajit and me. She saw

everything. It happened in our house. Baba was getting the first floor of the house constructed. The labourers had stepped out for lunch or maybe it was their day off, I don't remember. What I do remember is an extremely dusty floor. And I remember Ajit spreading a newspaper on it. I remember lying flat on my back on the newspapers. I don't know why she climbed those stairs. Was I shouting? Could she hear sounds? Whatever it was, she came up and saw it all. Ajit ran away. Aaji looked stunned, puzzled, and now that I think about it, even a little uncomfortable. She talked to me after that.

I remember this image so clearly. I was lying on the floor, the afternoon sun shining bright, filtering through her room. I was scared and enormously guilty. Ashamed of myself for getting caught doing things I knew I should not have been doing. She was sitting on her bed, asking me questions. What was happening there? Why was Ajit in the house? I told her. I told her everything I could, every bit that I understood of what had been happening to me. How I was often called to their house. How my clothes were removed. How he moved on top of me. How it hurt. She didn't tell me what it was. She didn't tell me anything. She could've told someone something. She didn't. She didn't make it stop. She did nothing. She didn't even tell me it wasn't my fault. Had she said those words, things might have been different. Had she said those words, I would not have looked so haunted in that picture.

3

If you do not tell the truth about yourself you cannot tell it about other people.

—Virginia Woolf

Aai

I AM MY AAI's carbon copy. So alike that if they made a film about our relationship, and I hope they do, both the roles will have to be played by the same actress. Just like in *Lamhe*, *Khuda Gawah* and *Nagina*, Sridevi's daughter was always played by Sridevi. I am Aai's daughter, always. And what a privilege it is, to look like my Aai. I have always had a hard time believing people whenever they told me I looked like her, because my Aai is beautiful. Her face radiates with a kind of beauty that hits you in warm waves of love. She is one of those people who moved others to break into song for her. When Aai was young and yet to become my Aai, she lived alone in another city. In the morning, she'd get ready and leave for work, and a boy in that gully whose voice resembled Mohammad Rafi's would croon, 'Nikla na karo tum saj dhaj ke, imaan ki niyat theek nahi.' As problematic as that might be in our modern-day context, it was considered romatic once. No one has, nor will, sing such songs for me. Which is why having her face is a privilege; it means that I might be beautiful too, like her. Even if just a little bit.

Aai and I have similar voices too. People often confuse me for her on the phone. It works well for me because then I can just hand over the phone to her, to seamlessly continue the conversation without having to engage in awkward small talk, the thought of which gives me anxiety. I have a hard time dealing with phone calls, anyway. They disturb me. Phone calls, in my head, are harbingers of bad news. But it's not just phone calls; I cannot handle the buzzing of the phone at all. Even the pinging of texts makes me jump out of my skin. The sound that my phone makes comes in the way of me processing my thoughts. It is why my phone is almost exclusively on the 'do-not-disturb' mode, and it makes Aai and Baba uncomfortable, especially when I am away from home. But I need my peace.

I'm so used to this silence now, it's almost hard to remember how different I once was. Was it really me, who'd get excited with the buzzing of the phone, especially at odd hours, because it came with the feeling of being wanted? Who enjoyed being in group conversations, who liked being remembered, who was comfortable being the centre of attention. My phone anxiety is tied to my generalised anxiety, of course. It is also, even though she won't believe you, another thing I got from Aai.

Aai has always been a worrier, always anxious about life, events however big or small. I should have noticed this, but children often take their parents and their presence for granted, something I have done too. Until recently, I didn't ever think about their mortality and what my life would look like if they weren't around anymore, so not noticing Aai's anxious tendencies was just a regular part of my cycle of ignorance. But now that Aai's mortality is something I cannot stop thinking about, now that I am more literate in reading the signs of change and distress, now that my own anxiety can't stop firing distress signals, I notice everything, I see everyone.

It had been a few days since Aaji's passing away. I was in Delhi, I hadn't gone for her funeral, but my brother had. Baba and Golu had gone to collect Aaji's ashes and Aai was alone at home. For the first time in her thirty or so years of marriage, she was completely alone in the house. The woman with whom she had had such a fraught relationship had finally breathed her last. Aai felt overwhelmed by how silent the house suddenly was and started hyperventilating. She started having trouble breathing. Maybe she even felt flutters of chest pain. Unable to understand what was happening to her, she went to the neighbour's house, in sheer panic. They took her to the doctor. At the clinic, they took her blood pressure. 150 over 93. It was high. The doctor then talked to her, asking what exactly was happening. By now, Golu and Baba were back. Aai had calmed down a bit. Her blood pressure was taken again. 130 over 85. The panic had passed. It wasn't a heart attack. So what was it?

When she told me about this episode, I knew she had had a panic attack. I knew because I, after all, was Aai's daughter. After having lived through several panic attacks, I was now equipped to understand what she was going through, and I would be able to help her if she reached out. I remembered all the times she told us she was feeling anxious about a train journey or a travel plan. How her stomach would give her so much trouble whenever she got anxious, how the two were eternally connected.

I told Aai that what she experienced was a panic attack; it could have triggers but not necessarily. I told her to see our family doctor about it and to maybe seek help from a therapist, or a psychiatrist. It was unlikely that she would, but I had to try. She didn't seek psychiatric help, but she did see our family doctor, Mishra uncle, and he prescribed her a Clonazepam variant for emergencies. Aai was also experiencing a period of insomnia for which she was given a minor dosage of sleep medication. As all this was happening, I was connecting the dots. All my health problems converged not just in Aai, but also Aaji, whose death had triggered this latent anxiety in Aai.

It was around this time that I wrote this poem mapping my Aai related inheritances. I am still too young to have unpacked all her gifts, especially the ones I am yet to receive. But much has already been given to me, and while I would have liked most of my presents to be material, this isn't too bad either.

Chocolate dipped worms are delicious

Being the older child of my parents
I shouldn't have been given hand-me-downs.
But there were always a few.
A wooden horsie that belonged to a cousin
was being passed down, generation after generation
like a prized possession.
Baba never had any siblings
except for a dead sister he never met
so he couldn't give me anything.
Just yesterday as he finished his daily routine
of morning exercise, he said to me,
I am sure I have given you something.
What? I'll find out soon.
Aai, on the other hand will never have trouble
recalling all her gifts to me.
She hands me her glucometer, and says, *Take it.*
The error margin is 15 per cent.
Always deduct that. Always.
Illness to me is a math test I know
I will eventually fail in.

Q&A

1. *Where do you get your terrible quality hair from?*
   Mother, of course.
2. *When Sridevi's daughter is born as Sridevi and marries the*
   man who wanted to marry Sridevi, what do you call it?

   A Freudian nightmare.
3.   *Where do you get your body weight from?*
     Mother, of course.
4.   *Do you think gluttony is a sin you should be killed for?*
     I like the floppiness of my body.
5.   *Can you list all your hand-me-downs?*
     Glucometer, wooden horsie, anxiety, candy doll, diabetes,
     kanjivaram saree, depression, and dental hygiene.
6.   *Why were you visited by a farting cat in your dream?*
     Scatological humour always works.
7.   *Which is your favourite hand-me-down?*
     Glucometer, of course. It's high-tech.
8.   *Is the farting cat funnier than Sridevi in* Chalbaaz?
     Of course.
9.   *Where do you get your hormonal imbalances from?*
     Mother, of course.
10. *When relatives come from abroad what do they bring?*
     Pringles, Twix candy, and condescension.
11. *Does the water in your house smell like someone dead?*
     It smells like Aaji.
12. *Do you think worms are our ancestors?*
     Chocolate dipped ones have the potential to be delicious.
13. *What happens when you eat your ancestors?*
     Genetic mutation.
14. *Are you a proud daughter of Aai?*
     Of course.

When I was five years old I started getting a peculiar pain in my left leg. It wasn't consistent, I wouldn't get it every day, but whenever I did, it would be without any reason. My left leg would hurt so much and so badly, I would cry. Aai, the biggest sceptic when it came to western medicine, would never let me take anything for the pain. They damage your liver, she'd say and take a dupatta or a piece of cloth and tie it tightly around my leg. She would then ask me to lie down on the bed with my legs up, resting against the wall. 'It will help with the blood circulation and your pain will be gone in no time.' The unscientific lies she made up to keep me distracted worked, at least on some nights. On other nights I would try to sleep and would eventually succeed. I'd wake up the next morning with the pain gone, and with red marks left behind by the tightly wound cloth knotted around my legs.

This pain, I realised much later, was a generational pain. Aai got it and Aai's Aai got it too. Maybe more women on my mother's side were prone to this unexplained pain, a legacy we were carrying with us, one that Aai wouldn't let me reject by simply taking a Paracetamol. Why find simple cures to your multi-generational problems when you can wear them like a cross, which I did, or a badge of honour which I do. I never really knew my Aai's Aai, my other Aaji, but this pain irrevocably links us. How can I then reject it, even if it comes in the form of suffering?

My only memories of this Aaji are set in poverty and illness. Aaji, of weak bones and sadness, was always falling and breaking some part of her body. Or she was crying. I remember her being in a cast. I remember her coming to stay with us and crying. I would wonder why she cried so much and how she didn't get bored of it. I'd tell Aai about it, and Aai wouldn't say anything. Whenever Aaji would come to stay with us, I wouldn't like it because she'd take my bed and she'd sit on it and cry. She was crying for her son who had walked out on her. She was crying for her daughter-in-law, the wife of her other son who she lived with and who was often cruel to her. I would listen to her laments and feel angry at the daughter-in-law, my Maami. But at the same time I would want her to go back. Perhaps that is the reason I cried so much when she died. I could never protect her, I could never be anything to her—not her granddaughter, not her saviour. My tears were not of sadness, but of self-righteous rage. It has taken me years to understand what she brought into my life—diseases, so many diseases, but also boundless love.

Every Saturday of my childhood, my Aai would drop me off at Aaji's place. Their house resembled the general compartment of a train, two rooms, one after another, both filled with misery and the stench of poverty. It was a house broken beyond repair, but everyone kept trying to fix it. It was the house of fat spiders and thin people, the house of porous walls, where you could hear everything the neighbours were saying, their every secret, all of their conspiracies. It was the house where Aai grew up, and I didn't. A house that Aai remembers fondly, and wonders how they never found it cramped for space, or why they never asked for more. My first lesson as a child came in that house; we don't give up on the people and spaces we love.

By the time I started visiting that house, most of Aai's sisters—she had four—were married. It was my Mama, Maami, Aaji, Azoba, and one remaining Maushi, who lived there. My cruel entitlement often got me in trouble in that house. This one story that has made it to the family legend, because everyone hated and continues to hate Maami, is a story I am not proud of.

Children are perceptive. They catch on to hostility as quickly as they catch on to love. Everyone hated the woman my Mama had married. Some of it was an organic hatred born out of the territorial nature of Indian families that want their kids to get married but don't want to share their love and affection with 'outsiders'. But my Maami was quite a mean cookie too, so I can't truthfully say she didn't deserve much of the disdain thrown her way. I wasn't asked to not like her, but I understood that the general opinion about her was not favourable and that gave me the sanction to be mean to her.

One Saturday, I was at their place as usual, having lunch with my two older cousins, my eldest maternal aunt's daughters. All of us were making faces and complaining amongst ourselves about the daal we had been served. I, the precocious child, not averse to cruelty, called for Maami. When she came out, I lifted my bowl of daal, poured it right over my plate, and with a smug expression looked at her and said, 'Daal kahan hai ismein?' Where are the lentils? My cousins and I had been bitching about it but I took it a step further, and made those two proud.

I should have been scolded for my behaviour. I was only five, but already a brat. I didn't deserve praise from my cousins for what I did, but that's just what happened. I saw fear on my Aaji's face and knew I had landed her in trouble. She hurriedly took me to the kitchen and whipped something up for me. I don't think I was ever given anything cooked by Maami after that. Aaji always made something for me till she could, and I ate it without complaining. I got along with everyone in that house except Maami. She didn't do anything to me to deserve my hatred. What I felt towards her was borrowed hatred. It was only later that I found out that she used to be abusive to Aaji, verbally and physically. And to her own children too.

In that all round tragic house where many of my Saturdays were spent, I don't remember talking to Aaji a lot. I remember her misery, and it's something I have carried into my adulthood. Aai's family was poor and could only break the cycle of poverty owing to their caste privileges and their hard work. Aai and most of her siblings got good government jobs and eventually made better lives for themselves. But most of the women of that household got Aaji's misery as an inheritance. Aai got all her illnesses. One of my aunts got poverty along with the illnesses. Yet another aunt got sadness in the form of an unhappy marriage with a philandering, abusive husband. They all suffered anguish in some form or another. Then how could I have escaped unscathed? Trauma, after all, runs in this family.

I was a cruel, happy and talkative child with a big secret. I was focusing my energy on escaping the things I had vowed to never talk about. I would often imagine a time when I would have to unveil my secret. It was always on my deathbed. I was always dying before everyone else and giving away my most guarded secret. None of this was easy. It took a toll on me and I acted out in unexpected ways, and sometimes people who had nothing to do with my life and its horrors, became the victims of my rage.

One time I had a petty fight with a friend. We'll call him Rohit. Rohit and I were always fighting over one thing or the other. Our fights were often physical, and we both used our nails a lot, for scratching each other, preferably on the face. Our parents were sick of our fights, but we were also inseparable. We'd fight, scratch each other, and quickly forget about it. Not this day though. I don't remember what we had fought about, but it was a big fight. He scratched my face, very close to the eye. I cried a lot and when I was running from his house to mine, I bumped into Ajit. He picked me up, took me inside his house, stopped me from crying. Took my clothes off.

I was more angry now, but didn't know what to do. So after Ajit let me go, I went back home. In our small garden was a rose bush. I thrashed my hands against the bush, the thorns cutting into my skin. I was now bleeding quite badly. I went inside the house, lay on the bed, and silently wept into the pillow, which was stained with blood along with my tears. When Aai and Baba saw me, they asked what had happened, as they cleaned my wounds and bandaged my hands. I blamed those injuries on Rohit. I told them he did it because I gave him a small scratch. I don't remember what followed. I think Aai scolded him. I think he cried. I think I felt guilty and apologised to him. I hope I did that.

Years later, I wrote this poem.

The Gift That Keeps Giving

My therapist thinks I am maladaptive,
when I tell him I sneak up on Aai
and check for her breathing
night after night.
One time when I was alone at home
watching television the way Azoba had
warned me against—for good reason—someone
walked into our house and never left.

The night of horrors remains etched in my memory.
A thief smiled at me, and stole our blind
tenant's hand bag. The next day she slipped
and cracked open her head.

Worms were eating her eyes from
the inside. They threw wet mud in
her skull and planted some apple seeds.
Some worms are nutritious for the soil.

When my Aai's Aai died, I was alone, dreading
she might insist on meeting me. She smelled
like water in her death, a deep blue scar
glistening on her forearm. She was hideous
like poverty, like stench of piss in government
hospitals. Aai recalls her Aai's apple cheeks,
her long hair, as we fight over a
made-up game of whose mother
is the prettiest. I think about her Aai's buck teeth

but don't say it out loud. I spare her feelings.
My therapist asks me, were you always this
sensitive? And I nod in agreement, vigorously.
I once cut my five fingers for revenge

and blamed them on a friend. He cried a lot
so I went to him and fed him snacks,
with my bandaged fingers. And told him horror
stories, sitting on his dead azoba's chair.

The time of the night, when I was alone with my thoughts
was the time when I could fully mourn my losses, even if
I could not understand them. One such night when I fell
asleep thinking about the same thing I thought about most
nights, Ajit forcing himself on me, I dreamt of my maternal
grandfather, who I knew had died hungry, eating a big meal
in our kitchen. He died when I was too young and I have
no memory of him—his voice, his habits… All I remember

is his sick, and often injured body. He was always losing his balance, always breaking his already weak limbs. And yet, I saw him now standing at my door and just staring at me. It was as if he knew what I was hiding. I woke up in a state of panic. My body was burning up with high fever.

This fever that suddenly gripped me at 3 a.m. that night, would continue to plague me for months. I would fail my first maths test—2 on 10—because of this fever and cry my lungs out, worrying Aai. My fever would turn into a kidney infection, making me believe that my death was imminent. Making me believe I had AIDS. I imagined the worst, I knew AIDS had no cure so I feared I was doomed to a painful death. I still carry the memory of that fear and it has given shape to other fears. From a simple stomach bug to cancer, I am scared of everything, all the time. But I am yet to reach the conclusion of what it is that I am really afraid of.

For instance, my phone anxiety makes me worry about calling even the closest of friends. But it also makes me worry about losing my phone. I am constantly checking my bag for my phone that I am sure is lost forever. It happens almost every other week that I am panicking about losing my phone that is right there in front of me. As I rifle through my bag, my panic makes it hard to find my phone and that leads to more panic. Usually I have to dump all the contents of my bag out, or get someone else to look for it. It's almost always there.

It is exhausting, this never-ending game of hide-and-seek. It was because of a nightmare that I understood my weird relationship with my phone. I saw my brother, whom I have come to love, and not just out of an obligation to love a sibling, being murdered by the actor Arjun Kapoor. There is no reason why a failing actor should bear the burden of my nightmare but that is exactly how it was. In my dream, I am informed of my brother's murder by Arjun Kapoor and five of his goony friends. Then I have sex (if I can even call it that) with Kapoor. I am being forced into it, as the other men watch us. I feel violated and I cry, resting my head on his chest. After he can't finish, he discards me, laughs and starts walking away. It is in that moment of rejection that it dawns on me that I may have lost my brother. I start looking for my phone and I can't find it. I look and I look and I look, but it's gone. Panic sets in and I have an anxiety attack within the dream.

When I woke up from the nightmare, it was 3 a.m. And that triggered more fear in me. This time, I had a panic attack for real, or maybe the one in my nightmare had been real too, which just means that I had two panic attacks, back to back.

The next morning, I told my brother about the dream. He said he wasn't surprised. It had to be a bad dream since Arjun Kapoor was in it. I laughed and suddenly realised what losing my phone meant to me. It meant losing people. It meant losing all contact with the world, the world I care about. Growing up, clinging on to my secrets, I was lonely. That lonely little girl still exists within me. There is no comforting her, and it is why even though my phone is always silent, like I'd want all my inner voices to be, it is valuable. It can disrupt the silence when it gets overwhelming. It tells me that I am not lonely, not really, and I believe it.

This belief is part of my inheritance too. My Aai is one of those people who choose to believe in things. She is a religious woman and believes that faith may be able to solve a lot of our problems, if we let it. I may not be a believer like her, but I have learnt to put my faith into things. Sometimes with much scepticism, sometimes without any.

I remember a holiday we took with my childhood best friend and her family. We went to Sikkim. We spent ten blissfully happy days there. I love the mountains. I love winter. You know that often asked question about beach or mountains? I would choose the mountains every time. But that does not mean that the mountains are always kind to me. I suffer from motion sickness and my time spent admiring the beauty of the hills is often punctuated with vomiting sessions. The problem with all the preventive medicine is that it makes you drowsy and you end up missing all the beauty surrounding you. Aai, on this trip, told me she had discovered a new trick to help me curb my vomiting without taking any medication.

She asked me to sit on a newspaper during the car ride. She said there are some chemicals in the paper ink that interact with your body and stop you from puking. This was the most unscientific and ridiculous theory I had ever heard. But I was so desperate to stop puking that I sat on the newspaper in the car on our first trip to a flower show in Gangtok. And I did not throw up. It was most definitely not because of the newspaper. There could be a thousand reasons why I didn't throw up.

Maybe the curves of the road weren't sharp enough. Maybe the air quality suited me better. Maybe it was the altitude, or the wind, or the lack of pollution. Maybe it was just the smiling faces of the people I came across. Anything but the chemicals in the newspaper. But I stuck to her remedy and did not vomit even once in those ten days I was in Sikkim.

Psychosomatic cures for psychosomatic pain. All made possible because Aai taught me to believe. Of the many things I have inherited from her—my body weight, my diseases, my poor quality hair, my willing smile, my pain and my resistance to pain—my faith is the one I hold on to the most. Aai, I know, can cure everything, my suffering included. It is why I am writing this book in my home, her space. Because I know there is no better place to do it than where Aai lives. She will get me through this, without knowing how.

Aaji

A few days back, right before I started thinking about this part of the chapter, formulating ideas and recalling stories for it, Aaji came to me in my dreams. My entire family was present, we were discussing an upcoming holiday and Aaji was sitting next to me on our old sofa—the big, cushiony, maroon, rexine sofa that was discarded much before I chose to discard parts of my childhood. Aaji's presence was marked by her anger at something, me most likely. She, in a quiet voice, said to me, 'When your grandfather died, he told you I love pineapples and yet you haven't brought me a single pineapple.' I had nothing to say, so I stayed silent and she continued, 'He also asked you to take care of me.' And then she walked away to my room that used to be hers when she was alive, and started looking at herself in one of the many mirror pieces she collected for reasons only she knew.

I woke up with a strange yet familiar feeling in my stomach. I knew what it was. Aaji was trying to manipulate me, trying to change the narrative. She wasn't going to stop me from writing about her, she was far too self-involved to ever miss the chance of being in this book. But she wanted me to write her with kindness. If you knew my grandfather, you'd laugh at Aaji for trying to use him and not my Baba. Azoba was a man of few and measured words. He'd never ask for kindness for his wife. He would never ask for anything. But, trust Aaji to play these tricks on me. So, I give in. You win for now, Aaji. I will write about you with kindness. I will begin with my most prized inheritance that I got from you—my love for books.

I know how much literature has saved me from myself and the world around me. It is a terrific joke the universe has played on me. The woman who was supposed to save me but didn't, ended up giving me the strength and the tools to unpack all my gifts, all my curses, even if unwittingly. Azoba, too, loved reading books, he would give me one book daily to read, and I would read it and return it to him, to be placed back in his bookshelf. But it was Aaji's secret obsession with literature, that trunk where she kept her *Chanda Mama* collection and read them in the afternoon when no one was watching, like they would take the books away from her, that made me fall in love with literature. It was something I needed to guard, save from prying eyes, not let anyone take away from me. Unlike Azoba, Aaji was possessive about everything—her books, her learnings, her failings. She never shared her books with me, not till I was old enough to handle them with the care they deserved. You just couldn't take anything, not even love, from her. Which is why I call my love for books an inheritance. It wasn't given to me out of choice, it passed on to me and there was nothing she could do about it. She couldn't have taken it back. I wouldn't have given it back either.

Ludwig Wittgenstein has this profound idea on the inability of saying things one wants to say but can't. He says, 'If only you do not try to utter what is unutterable then nothing gets lost. But the unutterable will be—unutterably—contained in what has been uttered.' When I first read this quote—and I have to admit I came to Wittgenstein through Maggie Nelson's piece-of-my-heart of a book, *Bluets*, for there is no better way of arriving at a writer and their thought, through another writer—I scoffed at Wittgenstein. What does he know about unutterable things, I thought. What does he know about the losses they bring into your life? Haven't I lost enough simply because I chose silence over mouthing my worries, my tragedies?

My losses, though, have appeared to me like wisdom, only in hindsight. When I was living through the horror stories of my childhood, they seemed to be a part of life. Yes, they were unutterable and remained unuttered, but that was a small fraction of the larger life I had, full of people who loved me, cared for me, played with me, respected me, wanted me. So, maybe, nothing changed as such. Maybe, nothing was lost as such. But that does not mean that the unutterable was not contained in whatever was being uttered. Aaji saw things happen to me, things that I should have been protected from, but because she chose inaction, my relationship with her was ruined without me even trying. In fact, I didn't know that our relationship was doomed.

I could never be kind to her, never happy with whatever she did for me. I criticised her cooking, frequently lashed out at her, and blamed her for her sexist attitude towards me. I thought she was nicer to my brother than she was to me, because he was a boy, which I now don't think was true at all. She was no sexist. I remember when others would frown upon my short dresses and skirts she'd only have good things to say. When I moved to Delhi and discovered 'fashion', she was the only one truly happy at seeing all my fancy and skimpy clothes. 'Bhowli sarkhi diste.' You look like a doll, she'd say. She encouraged and supported my education. While other colony aunties looked at me with suspicion, she tried to be friends with all my guy friends. She was probably extremely progressive and always kept up with the times, but she did prefer my brother over me. And why wouldn't she? He was the antithesis of me. He was always kind to her and willingly spent time with her, while I just ran away. But there's more to it, I think, than my running away. I will come to that bit too, but let me first take you through her story. After all, the unutterable is contained in these stories we tell.

When Aaji was not even ten years old, she lost her mother to an incurable illness whose name she didn't remember. She had once told me how beautiful her mother was, and how she loved my Aaji the way no one had since. It is because there was nothing better than a mother's love, she'd say. The perfect mother of Aaji's memories cooked all her favourite meals, bathed her and braided her long dark hair, before tying it with two bright red ribbons in the shape of a bow. She taught her how to wear a saree. And she died.

Aaji's mother may have taught her the essential art of draping a saree, but I always imagined little Aaji in a short floral frock like baby Neetu Singh in the film *Do Kaliyan*, singing, 'Bachhe mann ke sachhe'. Was she true of heart as a kid? I think she was. My imagination allowed Aaji to be the kid she didn't get to be for too long because her Aai died and she had to grow up too soon. She didn't talk much about her father, but whatever little she did say, I understood that he was a strict man with a busy work life. Busy enough to not pay attention to his only daughter, whom he shipped off to his sister.

She was called back when he remarried a year after his wife died, and gave Aaji a new Aai. I have always thought of Aaji as the Snow White of her own story. She lost a loving mother when she was very young. She was made to live with a stepmother who was perhaps kinder than the evil queen, but in a sudden turn of events, she too quickly passed away, handing over the two daughters she had borne, to Aaji. From a child to a woman, to a mother, in a matter of a few years—that was Aaji. And if you think her father showed her any kindness after that, you couldn't be more wrong.

Soon after the death of his second wife, he married again. My great-grandfather, whose name I do not know, was probably as afraid of loneliness as any of us. His third wife wasn't kind to Aaji or her sisters. When she, too, died, Aaji wanted to escape that house where death was a more permanent member than any of its women. Where, every time her father got her a mother, she was snatched away. Maybe, Aaji said, her mother's spirit was looking out for her and saving her from prospective cruelty, while subjecting her husband to the life of loneliness he was so desperate to escape. But I have my own ideas. It's not like I don't believe her talk of spirits, I do. Call me irrational, but I do believe they co-exist with us, I just don't think they interfere in our lives. I imagine they have their own interesting lives to lead. I think all those women died because they had to. Because that house wasn't going to let them live. Because women of a certain generation often died in silence, for they hadn't been allowed to find their own voice.

It is why I think Aaji lived such a long and healthy life. She had placed herself very neatly in the life of my father, her only son. He always heard her voice. He always listened to what she had to say, her voice, unlike the voices of her mother and stepmothers, was always relevant in this house. Unfortunately, like many women of that generation, who drew their self-worth from their family's dependency on them, she was also insecure of being replaced.

I don't have the exact timeline—people of that time weren't good at recording their personal histories—but Aaji's wedding to my Azoba happened soon after stepmother number two entered her life. From whatever little I know of her, she wasn't very nice to Aaji and her two half-sisters. However, the details of her bad behaviour remain sketchy. This evil stepmother could not have been much older than Aaji; it might have been my great grandfather's third marriage, it was her first. Therefore, I cannot really blame her for not being able to provide a motherly environment for my grandmother who was nearing adulthood.

This idea of the 'evil' stepmother is cemented in history. If one thinks about it, there are good mothers and there are bad ones, but stepmotherhood has been carrying the burden of villainy for eons. After all, our insecurities and anxieties and folklore and mythology have a co-dependent relationship, they borrow from each other. From Kaikei to Cinderella and Snow White's stepmother, our stories are full of these evil, conniving women. We are happy to typecast them, no one is really asking these mothers what their motives could be. They are already beyond redemption in popular imagination.

Stepfathers, like ordinary fathers, are kept at an arm's length from such discourses. Perhaps they are too busy for these petty domestic affairs. Not so the mothers though, because the baggage of sainthood has been put on their shoulders by every culture in different ways. We are almost setting up stepmothers for failure. The word, 'step' manages to alienate the new woman in our life. In Hindi it is 'sauteli maa', in Marathi 'savatrayi aai'. My grandmother was nearly an adult when this woman came into her life, and while there is no age for the need of a mother, this woman, a few years older than her, could hardly have fulfilled that role. Most likely this relationship had been thrust upon her without her permission. But within the domestic politics of motherhood, nature is always supposed to win over nurture, without any substantiative proof. Isn't motherhood the greatest achievement of a woman, after all?

So deep-rooted is this romanticisation of motherhood that there is an abundance of fantastical stories around it. Some stories even border on the supernatural and yet are unquestioningly consumed to keep this rhetoric going. A story my Aai often narrates is about one of her childhood friends, let's call him Arun.

Arun had a lovely, kind but sickly mother. She dearly loved her son and he loved her back. But then one day, her illness finally got the better of her. She died and was reduced to being a photograph on the wall. Arun, still pretty young, needed a mother figure and his father obliged my marrying again. But as is the fate of most stepmothers, she wasn't kind to Arun. She was nothing like his real mother. Aai never elaborates on her purported acts of cruelty and I suspect she herself may not know. Yet I believe the version of events simply because I know that Arun uncle wouldn't have lied about being abused, in whatever capacity, by his stepmother. Anyhow, this cruelty went on for a few years but then, according to Aai, this new mother started going a little mad. She would look at the photo of Arun's mother and blame her for all her troubles. She complained she was being haunted by her. Arun's mother had come back to save her son from an evil woman and wasn't going to rest till she neutralised the threat, Aai says with conviction.

The story doesn't end here. The presence of Arun's Aai's spirit drove the stepmother up the wall, and she got so preoccupied with her own fears that she forgot to torture Arun. The boy then grew up with his mostly good, if a little disinterested, father, the ghost of his kind mother, and the now mad evil stepmother. The kind-hearted person that he was, he took care of his mad stepmother till the very end. Now, as certain as I am that Arun suffered as a child, I also take comfort in knowing he was rescued. But there is no one to rescue the stepmother from the trap that everyone is just waiting for her to fall in. While stepmothers are generally considered suspect, 'real' motherhood is hardly, if ever, held up for scrutiny. And it is a political issue that each mother thinks she is beyond reproach, that she cannot make any mistake, that she always knows what is best for her child. Mother knows best, we are told over and over, till we believe it.

Aaji was an overprotective mother. I don't blame her for that, she almost had no choice. My Aaji did not marry my Azoba for love. It was societal obligation more than anything, she was of an age where it was expected that she would marry and go to her husband's house and take care of her new family.

They might have grown accustomed to each other's presence, and fallen into a habit of being around each other, but there was little more to their marriage outside of the roles society imposed on them.

Azoba was a man of very few words. On some days you could count those words on your fingertips. He preferred his books, his walks and his occasional indulgences. And he liked to sit in the sun. He liked it so much that, like a sunflower, he followed the sun, moving as the sun did. Depending on where the sunlight was the brightest, he would be found sitting in either our front yard, or our neighbours'. We had a comfortable chair for him, as did our thoughtful neighbours, so he could just sit and soak up all the sun he wanted and doze off peacefully. Our days were a lot less hot when he was around, I think, because he was absorbing all the heat for us.

Azoba used to wake up at four in the morning and leave for his morning walks. He would roam the city, lose himself in its streets and boulevards. He had no set route, he would go wherever his feet took him. There were days when I would spot him from my school bus, miles away from our house. He would already have walked for a few hours by then, and still be at least an hour away from our house. That was Azoba. His walks in the sun never tired him.

I would want to say that my Azoba was the first fair man I knew. But then I don't know how true that would be for everyone in my family. He was fair to Aai, and he was always more than fair to me, but I don't know what went on between Aaji and Azoba since they never talked, neither to each other nor about each other. So, whatever I say here is basically pieced together from conversations with my parents and relatives over the years. Azoba worked with the Accountant General's office, a job that made him travel a lot. He was closer to his friends than to his relatives, something he, thankfully, has passed on to me.

There was a time when Azoba's family—Aaji and my Baba—and Azoba's friend's family lived in the same house. Baba grew up with the friend's four kids and they became his siblings. Those siblings became my aunts and uncles, who loved me and my brother like one loves their real nieces and nephews. Relationships forged out of true respect and affection were always as important to Azoba as familial ties. This was the big learning that came to me through his actions. He was always teaching me things by handing me a puzzle that I would have to solve myself to get to the meaning. Like all the books he handed me without uttering a word about them, letting me decide what I wanted to learn from them, if I wanted to learn anything at all.

Aaji was the stark opposite of Azoba. She was a talker. She loved to talk, she talked so much and with such abandon that sometimes she didn't even need listeners. Many afternoons she would start talking to me and wouldn't stop even if I exited the room or the house. If Aaji was determined to finish a story, she would, with or without an audience. Not that I gave this behaviour much thought at all while growing up, but now I think she might have been trying to fill the silences in her marriage through her constant chatter.

Aaji and Azoba's strange relationship was how I thought most people aged into their lives. They didn't share words, they didn't share a bed, they didn't even share a room. Whenever I would go for sleepovers at my friend's place, I would always be surprised to see their grandparents retiring to the same room. It felt wrong, amoral. Grandparents weren't supposed to do that, they were supposed to draw boundaries, they were supposed to let their grandchildren sleep in their rooms.

The distance between them, the lovelessness in their marriage, was a norm of their time, I'd imagine. Which is why when someone had a love story, it was talked about for decades, and when someone didn't, it was just accepted. Their silent relationship was accepted without any questions raised in our house which is why it was easy to come up with imaginary inner lives for them.

For instance, I think Aaji filled the lack of passion and love in her marriage with other things like cinema and literature and conversations. Azoba's comfortable job ensured she had enough money to buy books, go for films with her friends and neighbours. He was a man of minimal needs, he needed his morning tea, his meals on time and that was all. He never bothered anyone with any demands, he didn't even have a favourite meal; he'd eat whatever you served him. If you were late in serving him his dinner, he simply would go to sleep without it, not out of anger, but because his routine was strict, or so he wanted us to believe. Though I caught him a lot of the times, in the middle of the night, sneaking quietly into the kitchen, looking for sugar to eat, and I looked the other way. Who was I to catch him out on his few indulgences?

Azoba, I know from Baba's stories, was gone a lot of the times, and Aaji was more used to his absence than his presence. I think this habit helped this silent marriage sustain. But his absence also made her rely on Baba more and more. His absence, and the fact that Aaji had already lost a daughter to a strange illness when she was only three.

She's Beautiful. She Will Die Soon

When your Aatya died… *Which aatya, Aaji?* When your Aatya died at the age of three, we already knew she was going to die. *Of course you knew, Aaji, you know magic.* It wasn't magic, it was black magic. She was a beautiful baby. Like the cherubs you see in churches? She was that beautiful. *Am I beautiful like the church cherubs, Aaji?* She was very beautiful. Everyone said so. It is why they let her die. *I don't want to be beautiful, Aaji. Then I won't have to die.* When she was two, our doctor looked at her and told us, you have been blessed with a healthy baby. She will die soon. When we found a matki broken in front of our house, we knew what was happening. *Was it magic that was happening, Aaji?* Black magic. She was so beautiful, it was out of our hands. *What happened then, Aaji?* She got sick. Really sick, and we saw everyone, we saw pundits, and aghoris, we took her to masjids and gurudwaras, they all told us the same thing. She's beautiful. She will die soon. *Why didn't you ask Gandhi ji, Aaji? He told Maushi she would pass her matric exams, and she did. He knows a lot of things, Aaji. Maushi said so.* She died soon. She died. I gave up my first born. *Can I see her picture, Aaji?*

Murphy Babies Always Die

You should never sit under a Peepal tree. It's haunted. You should never cross paths with a ghost either. If you see a ghost crossing a road, let him go first. Be respectful, he died before you were born. *But what if he died after I was born? Then can I go first?* When you cross a ghost your eyes become red. Your arms swell, and then they bleed. You get a high fever. Ask Bijju bhaiya. He once crossed a ghost's path and nearly died. *Is Bijju Bhaiya beautiful, Aaji?* Bijju was saved only because his Aai apologised to the ghost. Fed him good food. *Was the ghost hungry, Aaji?* He had so much fever. It would have reached his brain, and then he would have died. *Would he have become beautiful then, Aaji?* You know what happened to the Murphy radio baby? She, too, was beautiful. Look, look at her picture. *So beautiful.* Everyone wanted a Murphy baby. They wanted her so much but they couldn't have her. And so they killed her in their thoughts. If we can't have the Murphy baby, you can't either, they said. But I didn't. I already had my Murphy baby. Murphy babies always die. *Did she also cross a ghost, Aaji? Or was it magic?* What did I tell you? Murphy baby died because they all killed her. Her parents asked them not to. They said they will produce more

Murphy babies. *It would have been good no, Aaji? So many Murphy babies! Why can I not be a Murphy baby?* Murphy babies die the way Murphy baby died. *So I can never be a Murphy baby, Aaji? Her cheeks are so cute.*

One afternoon, Aaji told me about the daughter she lost. Her and Azoba's first born. I knew from Aai and Baba's stories that Aaji had some medical issues that led to a few miscarriages. The trauma of losing children whose bodies were yet forming within her was not any less than a stillbirth may have been. It had to be hard because she wanted children. When at last her wish was fulfilled and a child was born to her, she was snatched away too soon. And she lived her entire life under the shadow of that pain.

Aaji believed black magic killed her daughter. Why, she asked me, would a perfectly healthy child just die otherwise? I just sat there and nodded. It was a rare moment in my relationship with Aaji. She was opening up to me, sharing her past traumas with me. I was far too young to understand much, but I remember wanting to cry for the Aatya I would never meet, the Aatya who would have loved me so much had she been alive. But no tears came. Instead, I went to my study table, took my diary, and made a note: 'I will always be nice to Aaji from today. She lost a baby.' It felt good writing that, like I had proven to myself what a great person I was. I wanted others to know of my, yet unrealised, kindness. I was going to be kind and compassionate to Aaji, even though she may not reciprocate the kindness. I remember telling Aai about the Aatya I had lost, assuming she wouldn't know such family secrets. I told her I had decided to not fight with Aaji from that day onwards. She just smiled and told me it was the right decision.

Despite all my good intentions, my fights with Aaji never stopped. In the tussle between compassion and childhood cruelty, the latter often ends up winning. And what do little girls with perfect lives, like I imagined I had, know about loss? Aaji and I continued our battles, our big and small squabbles. I didn't like the fact that she openly favoured my brother over me. And I certainly didn't like the fact that she wasn't kind to my Aai. I remember a particular incident about this very clearly.

One afternoon, I came back from school, exhausted. The walk from the bus stop to our house, an easy stretch of 2 kms, was made difficult by the summer heat and the weight of the school bag on my shoulders. I was tired, thirsty and irritable. When I entered the house, I saw Aaji deep in conversation with a neighbourhood friend of hers. The two of them stopped the second they saw me. Aaji's friend gave me a smug smile and asked how my day at school had been. I dropped my bag in a dramatic fashion. I was in no mood for polite chitchat. I had already heard them bitching about Aai, something about her not caring enough about the house and being cruel to Aaji, things that I knew to be categorically false.

I glared at Aaji, turned towards her friend, and told her to leave right away. I didn't stop there. I told her she was not allowed to come back to my house because she was evil and said mean things about Aai, and pushed Aaji to do the same. 'Leave!' I thundered. It took Aaji a whole minute to recover from what I had done. She yelled at me, asked me to apologise, but this Bollywood-loving granddaughter of hers had consumed too much cinema to know that it was too late to back down. I had to stay committed to what I had just done. Undeterred, I asked her to leave again. The woman, probably embarrassed and maybe happy to have collected new gossip, left after telling my Aaji not to worry too much, I was just a child after all. What she didn't know was that I was already on my way to becoming the person I would continue to be all my life. I never saw her in our house again. Aaji didn't speak to me for several days after this incident. She probably wanted to punish me, wanted to complain to Aai and Baba about my errant ways, but she could not. It would require her to tell them everything that had transpired, and that would definitely reflect way more poorly on her, than it would on me. She therefore resorted to silence and everyone just assumed she was in one of her moods.

It took me several years to understand that the politics of domesticity in our house wasn't just that, it was defined by Aaji's undiagnosed PTSD which was slowly making her paranoid, more and more each day. My own PTSD diagnosis made me realise that Aaji had too much trauma in her life for her to not suffer from its consequences. It was during many of my therapy sessions in which I talked about Aaji and what she did and didn't do that I started understanding how she might have been suffering in ways that she didn't understand. And we didn't either. We didn't understand psychiatry then. It wasn't like we talked about our feelings with each other much, or discussed how the death of a daughter was still a matter of grave importance, pun unintended, after half a century of its occurrence. Remember I said I'd tell you about why I think she didn't save me? Why I think she and I never really got along well?

When Aaji's wedding was fixed to Azoba's, I imagine they didn't meet each other. They only met during one of their wedding ceremonies or pre-wedding ceremonies. I don't think they talked to each other. That is not how things worked in those times for most people. My grandparents weren't romantic, and they certainly weren't marrying for love. If you ask me, I don't think they ever fell in love. Love for them was more of an obligation, a fondness for the other person's presence in their lives, maybe. Or perhaps not even that. Just a habit, then.

I don't think they ever spoke of things like love or their feelings for each other. Rather they went about their lives the way they were supposed to, performing their marriage for the world. Aaji's transition from her maternal home to her house with Azoba was more a natural progression of life. She went from taking care of her sisters and father to taking care of Azoba. It would be unfair of me, though, to reduce Aaji to the woman who simply did the cooking, cleaning, and bearing the children part of domesticity. There was so much more to her.

Aaji, in her youth, was free spirited and emotionally independent, though her independence faded with age. She was the kind of woman who had many interests, and none of them were domestic, which made her an anomaly in that generation. She did handle the responsibilities that were thrust upon her well, but she didn't enjoy them. She didn't like cooking and was a horrible cook till the end of her time. She followed no major cleaning rituals, if the house looked clean, it was good enough for her. Everyday chores held no value for Aaji. So long as no one was hungry, it was fine.

If she were a young woman today, I feel she would've fit right in. Her interests, if you ask me, were too avant garde for her time. She loved to read, watch films and talk. It wasn't her love for these things that made her different, but how fiercely she protected her love. She would save enough from the money that Azoba gave her to run the household for her books and movies. Azoba's job also kept him away for long periods which meant the house was often quiet. Aaji, who was so used to Azoba's silent company, probably didn't really mind. We are all creatures of habit after all, and she was, by then, used to Azoba's quiet company. He was born with that profound silence and nothing and no one could break it. For him, meeting a friend meant sitting together and reading a book. In all my childhood photos with Azoba, you can sense that deep and peaceful silence on his face and you can see it on mine too. Pictures of me, when I was a one-year-old baby or when I was ten years old, reflect back the silence.

Children are perceptive and absorb whatever you give them. Azoba's legacy to me has been his silence.

Within the boundaries of Azoba's silent presence and vacant absence, Aaji built her life, filled with books and evening movie shows. Azoba was a man of basic needs so he let his wife be, however she was. He wasn't the kind to bring guests unannounced, expect his wife to cook all the time or even make any extravagant demands. Nor did he mind Aaji going out on her own with friends, men and women. He was a bit ahead of his time, if I may say so. The marriage was harmonious for a while, I think. By the time, I witnessed their relationship, the rhythm had been disrupted, and they were no longer singing the same song. There weren't any fights or ugly words, but there was a simmering resentment between them.

Azoba's silence was so permanent that it didn't break even when his daughter died. It wasn't because he didn't love her, but because he didn't know how to express things the way Aaji could—be it love, be it his sense of loss. The death of a child is hard on any marriage and it's not outrageous to assume that it was so on this one too. When Aaji lost her first child to a mysterious ailment, it took a toll on her body. I don't think her body was ready to let go of her child any more than her soul was. Whenever she and Azoba tried to have another child, Aaji miscarried. Almost like her body was still grieving the loss of the first born and couldn't see another child taking her place. Grief works in strange ways.

Because so many children had missed the chance of being raised in Aaji's arms, when Baba came into this world, she latched on to him. She held him tightly, with love, with fear, never wanting to let go of him. And she didn't, not till her last breath.

This love is the beginning of my tragedy.

Aaji's love for Baba was blinding. She was never comfortable with the idea of Baba being shared by anyone. Tied by conventions, when she went looking for a bride for Baba, I hear that she rejected many women at some slight pretext or the other. It's not that she didn't want Baba to get married; marrying her son off to a suitable bride was what society expected of her. It was a ritual to be followed and she did not stop to question it. It was only when the wedding finally happened did she realise how uncomfortable she was with another woman's presence in the house. She wasn't prepared for how much Aai's presence would irk her and she began acting on her bafflement in the age-old way— by being hurtful towards her daughter-in-law. She would often unfavourably compare Aai to other women whose proposals she had once turned down. She seemed to imply that she had not made the best choice. The truth is, no woman with whom she had to share her son could've escaped her wrath.

During the early years of Aai and Baba's marriage Aaji tried to interfere in their relationship a lot. She wouldn't let them go out for movies or dinners alone, making it clear that she expected to be invited.

On one occasion, Baba had gone to pick up Aai from my maternal grandmother's house. On their way back, they decided to watch a movie before returning home. When they reached home after their stolen evening together, they met with Aaji in her Lalita Pawar glory—furious and with one eye twitching in rage. She was sitting in the living room, frothing with hatred. Aaji slept hungry that night, only because my parents, both adults, had decided to watch a film on their own.

Aaji would often keep Baba up late, and wouldn't let him retire to his room by coaxing him into watching late night television shows or engaging him in conversations. She would make Aai wake up at 4 a.m. to make tea for herself and Azoba who would, then, leave for his walks. These sly machinations ensured that Aai was tired early and slept before Baba could retire to their room. And that ensured there was no intimacy between the two.

This charade went on for a while but even she could not have kept it up. Baba at some point had to find his voice and I suppose he did. Or else I would not have been born. And this is how my tragedy is interconnected to Aaji's obsession with Baba.

Aaji walked into that under-construction room some twenty-six years ago, saw Ajit assaulting me and simply walked away. Ajit pulled up his pants and ran away in panic. She didn't offer me her hand to pull me up from the ground. I had to get up on my own, dust my frock, fix it, and walk back to my room alone, guilty, ashamed and terrified. Later that day she asked me what had been happening and I told her all that I could. She nodded and didn't say or do anything. Not one reassuring word, not one promise.

The matter of her not taking any action despite knowing this horrible truth, has haunted me time and again. Why didn't she do anything? Who was stopping her? Did she really not care about me? A few years later, when all of this had ended, when I was used and abandoned by Ajit, our extended family went on a holiday to the northern hills. Aaji and Azoba were asked to join us but they declined. 'Take me to Kashmir when you go there', said Aaji and we agreed. Baba was worried about his old parents being in the house alone, especially at night, and so he asked Ajit if he could spend the night at our place. He agreed. By this time, my undoing was well behind him. It was like nothing had happened between us, Aaji had seen nothing; he had done nothing. Like the cement on my frock that afternoon, this too was done and dusted.

Aaji had continued to dote on him. After we returned from our holiday, Ajit told us how Aaji would wake up in the middle of her sleep to make tea for him. He was preparing for his engineering exams. He needed the tea to stay up. I laughed at the story. I laughed at the fact that she never, not once, made anything for me, never heated a single chapatti for me, never ever asked if I had eaten my lunch.

I was the living proof of my parents' relationship. I was the proof that another woman had replaced her. I, who looked way too much like the other woman, was worthy of her contempt. The year she died, old, frail and senile, I didn't go for her funeral. I couldn't. But that year we took a trip to Kashmir, the only place she ever wanted to visit. It wasn't planned, so make of that what you may, but I now know I went to Kashmir to free myself of her burden. I used that pained heaven on earth, much like every Indian, to heal myself.

PART III

1

When they asked me what I wanted to be I said I didn't know.
'Oh, sure you know,' the photographer said.
'She wants,' said Jay Cee wittily, 'to be everything.'

—Sylvia Plath, *The Bell Jar*

I AM BEGINNING THIS chapter with a quote from *The Bell Jar* because this book came to my rescue when I found myself drowning in the depths of depression for the first time in my life. And because in that part of my life I did want to be everything.

This part of the story introduces you to the twenty-two-year-old M who was a romantic who fell in love easily and who cared about people. Who thought nothing was impossible, who thought she could do anything. Who was at the brink of her first serious heartbreak and inches away from fully realised depression. Who was going to fall irreversibly in love with literature, which would come to her rescue, time and again.

This is not one of those memoirs where the writer lives a hard life, but escapes it all by getting a scholarship to study in Oxford or Harvard. For that read Jeanette Winterson. I barely managed to scrape through my class 12th board exams, got through a perfectly mediocre college in Jabalpur and completed my engineering with good enough marks. I did not sit for any campus interviews because I didn't want a job, I wanted to figure out my life. As my friends prepared to leave our hometown—some for the US to pursue their Master of Science in Engineering, others to join IT companies—I sat at home.

I would take a gap year to read books, watch the news and educate myself about the world, or so I told myself. Aai and Baba were disappointed but tried to hide it. I read books and watched the news, but mostly I spent my time on the internet, giving my unsolicited and absolutely half-baked opinion on everything to whoever was listening. The year was 2009 and the news of Telangana demanding statehood was all over the internet. I found I had opinions on the subject that I wanted to make known.

I joined a few forums on Facebook, where young boys and girls from Andhra Pradesh wrote many righteous updates about why this separation would destroy the unity of the state. There was strength in unity, they said. Any concerns that the Telangana supporters had could be addressed if they stood together. I had no stakes in this game. But now that I had already allowed myself to get pulled into the hard-to-escape spiral of internet debates, I wanted to feel valid. I read up on the Telangana issue and armed with my Wikipedia research, dove deep into these debates. Internet is floating with lonely millennials trying to find their place in the world, putting their feet where they don't belong, fighting for causes they don't know anything about, all from their comfortable armchairs. I was an armchair activist in the truest sense. What did I understand of Telangana's suffering? The validity of its demand for statehood or the lack of it thereof? It was just a hot topic in news those days and I was free. I was also lonely. My friends had moved cities. I wanted people to engage with. And because I thought I was a political person, this felt like not just the right but an important cause to participate in. And participate I did. So much so that I would often be called by the forum admins of all the Telangana groups I was part of to put forward my unbiased and 'totally valid' opinion. So that I was taken seriously, I even pretended that I had first-hand experience of something similar. I had seen Chattisgarh being ripped out of Madhya Pradesh and knew of the ensuing pain, I claimed. It was all lies.

Why did I do it? In my family, we discussed politics but it was all about practical issues that concerned us. We weren't really concerned with the history of abuse, or the many political revolutions taking place within our state borders. But when has the lack of understanding of the world stopped young people from having an opinion about it? Didn't Oscar Wilde once say he wasn't young enough to know everything? Well, I was. And I knew everything. These political debates were exhilarating for me. I felt seen and heard. Even when I was abused on these forums, I would tell myself it was because I was saying things no one wanted to hear, the hard things.

Some members of our Facebook group went on television debates, argued with Telangana politicians on live television. We all clapped and cheered for them when we watched the news clips. There were petitions made and my name was added to them without me having to say anything. I felt like I belonged. Today, I wonder if most of us knew what we were fighting for, because I certainly didn't.

When Telangana was finally carved out of Andhra, everyone in the group was dismayed. I was sad too, but it was more for myself than the cause we had failed. This group, where I had been spending all my days and most of my nights, engaged in misguided fights with those already oppressed, had changed something in me. I understood what it was like to belong, to have your opinion matter. Now that the group was dissolving and people were moving on with their lives, I had to figure out what to do with my life too.

My engineering days were over. Encouraged by my recent political engagements, I decided I wanted to be a journalist. This would be my world, where my opinions would matter. My general knowledge was reasonably good and my English was decent. I knew securing an admission to journalism school would not pose a problem. I applied to the Asian College of Journalism, touted to be one of the best journalism schools in the country; The Indian Institute of Mass Communication (IIMC); Indian Institute of Journalism and New Media (IIJNM); Xavier's and a new school called School of Convergence.

My admit card for the IIMC entrance exam got lost in the

mail. By the time it arrived, it was too late for me to sit for the exam. But I did write the ACJ, IIJNM, and SoC exams, and cleared all three. Next, I cleared the interview round in all three colleges. I could pick where I wanted to study. In what would traditionally be considered a bad decision by most, I opted for School of Convergence. They were offering me a scholarship, which was an important factor. Also, I felt like Chennai, where ACJ was situated, was too far from Jabalpur and I would not be able to make quick trips back home, whenever I wanted. Besides, I had always wanted to go to Delhi. The national and political capital of the country would be the place where I'd write my destiny. I had made up my mind. Despite what everyone said, I went to Delhi and started my new life there.

Delhi, my first home away from home, would soon grow on me like a vine, wrapping itself around me, trapping me in its lush, green embrace. Soon, this city would introduce me to a new side of myself. In its hot, sweaty summers and harsh, cold winters, I would endlessly stumble upon myself. In its minars and forts, that I would look at lustfully, I would find my soul sinking and re-emerging. It was a piece of history that was so impersonal and yet so all-consuming. I would find a house with a view of the Qutub Minar, where I would sit in my balcony, just looking at its magnificence. I would wonder at how it was visible even from afar, and how I too was visible from afar, but looking at me from a close distance was bound to make anyone dizzy.

Delhi would also teach me to not reduce myself to a

monument. In Delhi, I met some people who would shape my life in ways that I am certain, without much evidence, Chennai could not have. Not that city, but that school had a competitive spirit that was sorely missing in Delhi. It gave me the space to bloom, gave me friends I would keep in my life, never to let go. Form what I think are lifelong bonds. Delhi would encourage me to talk about my past. It would teach me to engage and disengage. It would introduce me to a writing professor who would make me fall in love with writing and change my life forever.

I know all logic says I should have regretted my poor decision of leaving a reputed, fancy college and choosing the one I did. My parents still question my decision. When I tell people about the decision I made ten years ago, they assume I'm regretful. On discovering I am not, they question my choice with much indignation. I do understand their surprise. Had I gone to Chennai, it's very likely I would have had a stable career by now. I would have worked with leading media houses, perhaps changed jobs a couple of times; I would have been making good money. I would've been a success.

People don't know of the price I would have to pay for this success though. Poetry, in all probability, would not have happened to me. I would not have met my friends and talked about my childhood with them. And this book would never have happened. Had I gone to Chennai I would have not met Eric, my professor who pushed me towards writing. Whose essay exercises taught me how to look at the world differently. He was the first teacher of my life to have this profound, life-altering influence on me, who showed me I had talents I didn't know existed. Had I moved to Delhi later, it would have been a different city for me. Not my first home, not the city where I sat and cried over all the petty fights that came with adjusting to a new life. It would not be the city where I would come of age. Not the city where I would repeatedly find and lose love.

As much as a city changes you, you change the city too. Each city means different things to different people. My Delhi was a sanctuary where I could become the person I am. It is because of the harshness, the pollution, the love, the fear, the beauty it subjected me to that I found everything I value in life today.

I moved to Delhi in August 2010 and in November I went home for a week to attend my childhood friend Neha's wedding. I am not really a wedding enthusiast but I was excited about this one. Neha and I became friends when she came to stay with her uncle, who lived in our neighbourhood. When we were in the sixth standard, her parents returned to Jabalpur and she moved out of her uncle's house to live with them. That is when she met Rohan, the guy she was about to marry. Like in any good romantic story, he was the friendly boy next door. They soon fell in love. A decade or so later it was time for them to tie the knot, and I had to be there as the first witness of their love story, and as the bride's best friend.

I landed in Jabalpur, bang in the middle of chaotic wedding preparations. In the midst of this celebratory mood, I got a call with some terrible news. One of our close friends,

Aditya, had lost his mother to an accident. He was pursuing his Masters in the US and was not in the country at the time of the accident. I knew how close he had been to his mother, and how this news must've been devastating for him. This is a fear many of us live with. I have spent much of my adult life trying to translate the fear I feel at the prospect of losing my parents into poetry. I know that Avi, who never got along with his mother, will be distraught when she dies. It's the nature of the relationship.

As the magnitude of Aditya's tragedy struck me, I decided I would be the support he needed to help him through this difficult time. The first thing I did was to call him. What do you say to someone who has just lost his mother? All words feel empty. Asking him how he was coping did not feel right but I desperately wanted to know if he was doing okay. I started with that. He was silent for a bit and then said he was fine. He was in Delhi where his mom was cremated. Bringing her body back to Jabalpur didn't feel like an option for them. Aditya would come to hate Delhi later for this reason.

A few days later, he and his family were back in Jabalpur. I was busy with Neha's wedding preparations, but I had to meet Aditya. It was the day of her mehendi ceremony. I told Aai I would first meet Aditya and then come to the wedding venue directly. Aai was aghast—I hadn't washed my hair yet, I wasn't wearing proper festive clothes and instead of getting ready, I was going to meet Aditya. After assuring her and Neha that I would be back in time to get mehendi designs done on my palms, I took out my Activa and left for his place.

Aditya looked sombre but better than I had expected. He asked me to inform his girlfriend and other friends about his mother's passing, he did not have the strength to do it. I agreed. I spent some time with him and then left for the mehendi. When I reached the venue, Aai was already there. She was furious that my hair looked so dirty and matted, and that I had come to a wedding straight from a house that was mourning a death. She was displeased with the clothes I was wearing, that I was choosing grief over happiness. 'Didn't Neha need you today?' she kept repeating. Why could she not see that Neha was happy, that she was marrying the man she loved. Aditya had lost his mother. Those who are happy don't need us the way those who are struggling do.

I met Aditya one more time before Neha's wedding. We talked about nothing because there was nothing to talk about. We sat in silence and drank our coffees. He told me he would not be returning to the university; I half-heartedly tried to urge him to go back. I knew he eventually would. As days would turn into weeks, he would realise he could mourn anywhere. And that is what happened.

After Neha's wedding, I went back to Delhi and life resumed. I had assignments to do, friends to make, a city to explore. And I had Aditya to take care of, even if he was far away and not really my responsibility. He had returned to the US. He had called me from Chicago, where he had a long layover and time to kill. His girlfriend had left him, he said. She was angry that he didn't choose her to be his companion in mourning, that he didn't call her once and left the country without meeting her.

She's a heartless bitch, I told him, but internally I smiled. He had called me and met me before leaving the country, did that mean I was more important? It didn't matter that his girlfriend lived in a different city and it was easy to meet me. Truth be told, I would have gone to Jabalpur just to meet him. That was a time in my life when I wasn't aware of all that was ailing me. Difficult days were just bad days that one had to overcome. Anxiety was fear that would go away on its own. I wasn't suffering with consciousness, and that made a world of difference. I could willingly offer my time and compassion to Aditya.

I had my studies and I had Aditya. Where was the time to think about anything else? We would spend hours talking to each other every day. I would sleep little and give him all the time I had. There was a day when we were on the phone for eight hours straight. He was possibly filling up his time, talking to me, so he wouldn't have to think about his dead mother. I was trying to find a place in his life because I was desperate for love. Back when we were friends in Jabalpur, he would often come and spend all day at my place, just chatting. This wasn't new for us. What had changed was his drinking. He would often be drunk when he was on the phone with me. I felt responsible for his well being, as if I was his surrogate mother, as if it was my responsibility to keep him happy, keep him well.

Soon our conversations started slipping into territory that wasn't strictly platonic. We were beginning to straddle the lines of romance and friendship. I was already halfway there. I was so involved in taking care of him that I was beginning to forget myself a little. I desperately wanted him to acknowledge how selflessly I was taking care of him. How I was the one, the only one, who cared for him. I did really care for him. I was genuinely worried for him. Aditya was drinking heavily, he was popping any pill that would help him sleep. He was dealing with a major life trauma and didn't know how to handle it. Intoxication and sleep were the only two ways he could block out the reality. He would drink a lot of whiskey, call me and cry, or flirt, and I would take both those things as a sign of the love that would one day blossom between us. I was delusional. He was sad and drunk. No good would ever come of it, but that did not stop me.

One night, Aditya called saying he hadn't been able to find any meds and was desperate for some sleep. Would I sing for him? Now, I do love to sing but I am a bathroom singer at best. But a drunk Aditya was the sweetest thing ever. He told me my voice was soaked in honey, and if he could just hear me sing it would comfort him and make him feel good about his miserable life, it would help him sleep. I happily gave in and sang, 'Abhi na jao chod kar, ke dil abhi bhara nahi'. Sahir Ludhianvi, the sad lonely lover just like me, wrote this beautiful song about love and heartbreak. I remember Shahrukh Khan had once mentioned it in an episode of *Koffee with Karan* and called it the most romantic song ever written. The twenty-three-year-old me knew better than to question Shahrukh's taste. So, I sang this song to Aditya, as my roommate smiled at me with adoration. The things one does for love. Aditya fell asleep without disconnecting the call, I also went to sleep with the phone still on call. The phone companies could cut the call for us if they liked, but we would not be ruining that moment.

Aditya was grieving and doing everything to survive the emotional crisis he found himself in. This included relying on me with full force, taking up all the emotional space I was willing to offer. He was not thinking about giving anything back to me and I thought that was okay. One day, I would be rewarded for this selflessness, but that day never arrived. On Valentine's day, that year, Aditya called me to tell me he wanted to kiss me. It was yet another drunken admission, but I was flying that day, singing, 'Aaj kal paav zameen par nahi padte mere.' My feet were barely touching the ground. If anyone had seen me at the metro station that day, they would have noticed the spring in my step. I was jumping, I was floating and I could not stop smiling.

I decided that I was ready to tell Aditya I was in love with him. I had no expectations of hearing it back from him. I knew he was sad, he was still in mourning. I just wanted to let him know that whenever he was ready to come out of this grief, I would be there, waiting for him. I drafted an email and sent it to him. He responded almost immediately, saying he didn't think he was the right one for me. I was too kind, too wonderful a person, and didn't deserve someone like him, in fact I deserved better. It was heartbreaking to hear those hollow words of compassion and pity. He didn't want to upset me, so he softened the blow by saying I deserved better. In retrospect, I wish he had just said no. It would have given me the clarity I deserved and saved me a lot of the hurt that he was trying to shield me from.

He may have refused my love, but he wasn't ready to let go of me. He was scared that if he turned me down completely, I would leave. I wasn't ready to let go of him either. I was afraid he was going to end our conversations because of my stupid and ill-timed confession of love. We were hanging on to each other in desperation. But how long could it last? It had to end one day, and it did when his ex-girlfriend came back into his life. They had been talking for months, but Aditya had neglected to tell me about it. One day, while talking, he turned on me angrily. He told me he had been trying to build his life back with her, but I kept coming in the way of that by constantly interfering in their relationship. I was confused and upset at being blamed for ruining a thing I did not know existed. I cried my eyes out on the phone and never spoke to Aditya again.

That was when my love affair with literature actually began. As I've said before, I was always a reader. I grew up reading as many books as I could find in my small town. But I had never read Sylvia Plath, Anna Akhmatova, Wislawa Szymborska, Helen Oyeyemi, Dostoevsky, Nabokov, Ondaatje. I never knew or understood sadness the way I wanted to understand it now. I needed a companion in my grief to mend my broken heart. For that, I turned to Plath.

This was also the time I became conscious of the fact that I could be depressed. What better cliché than falling in love and experiencing heartbreak to realise that you might be depressed? However, the fact that my depression might run deeper than a boy who could not love me, would take me a little longer to understand. After Aditya and I stopped talking, I dove right into literature. One of the biggest benefits of living in the national capital is the cheap books that you get there. Every nook and corner of the city has book vendors. Delhi has some great book stores—from Midland and Bahrisons to Spell & Bound, which now has shut shop. All these beloved shops stocked an incredible number of books. But most of all, I was grateful for the small time second hand book vendors. The Sunday book bazar in Daryaganj, that has now been shut on the orders of the High Court, as well as the book stalls in the PVR Saket complex, sold cheap books and had an incredible collection. And of course, there is the universal 'enemy' of the small guy, Amazon, my publisher. There were tonnes of books to buy and read, that would help me get over Aditya.

During my engineering days I was the person people would come to for book recommendations. I had read almost all the books in the small library of which I was a member. The librarian uncle, whenever he got any new books, would ask me to read them. He would then, based on my review of the book, place it either in the front, wanting other people to borrow it, or at the back. But this was a different phase. I was now actively seeking books as companions. I used to read for leisure, for the love of reading. Now I began reading to feel less lonely.

The Bell Jar was my first companion in this journey of self-discovery. Aditya's exit from my life had triggered something. I began with being sad which is common for any breakup, but what I was going through was more than sadness. I retreated into myself. I wondered what it was about me that he could not love. The first thing that came to mind was that I was fat.

No one stays with the fat girl, I kept thinking. When I had started my relationship with him, I had also started trying to lose weight. It is something you do when you are in love. Love as a thin girl would be easier, I would often say to myself. I had started eating oats for breakfast, something I absolutely hated, but gulped down with water. I stopped eating oats when my PG uncle very cruelly asked me if I was in love. Only love could make me lose weight, he said. I felt exposed. I felt my shallowness was displayed for everyone to see. The next day I stopped eating oats. There was time to lose weight, I said to myself.

But when Aditya left me that old feeling came back. This would never happen to a thin girl. This was also the time I had started talking to friends about my child sexual abuse experiences. I knew I was fat. I knew why I was fat. I was broken. I had been broken by men and I had let myself gain weight so I could hide behind my flab. I had wanted to become unworthy of touching, and the fact that Aditya had left me was a testament to my success. I was grotesque. No one wanted to touch me. Not even the man who had known me for years and turned to me when he needed help. And who had then discarded me.

This was where Plath came in. 'The silence depressed me. It wasn't the silence of silence. It was my own silence.' I wrote down her words in my journal. Each sentence of the book felt like it was written for me, with me in mind, like she was trying to reach out to me. Plath was beautiful. Plath was how sad women were supposed to look—fragile, broken and breathtaking. I was none of those things. It was why I was abandoned. How many sad, fat girls do you know who are considered beautiful or glamorous enough to be represented in popular culture? None. Not one. If there is no beauty in sadness, what good is it? That didn't mean Plath's sentences could not help me, of course. It wasn't her fault that she was beautiful and I was ugly. She, after all, was trying her best to help me.

It was in one of those dense-with-melancholia afternoons that poetry came to me. I woke up from a state of deep slumber. My eyelids still heavy with sleep, dried up tears I had fallen asleep to crusting the corners of my eyes, I picked up my journal and furiously scribbled my first poem. Then the second and the third. Three poems written in succession, one after the other. My writing journey had just begun and I had Aditya to thank for it.

Schizophrenia

My hundred-and-sixteen-year-old grandmother talks of a friend called Mary. Mary, she says, was the most beautiful woman she had ever seen. She had met Mary at her father's funeral and had become friends with her. It wasn't possible to not be friends with Mary. My grandfather, who sits on his rocking chair and stares at the clock, counting time, says that Mary does not exist, he has never met Mary. When my grandmother died at a hundred and twenty six, her last wish was to be buried at the cemetery where she had first met Mary. I dug the grave myself, while Mary watched me all the time, sitting on a neighbouring grave. How splendid you look, dear Mary, I told her; you are indeed the most beautiful woman I have ever seen. My grandfather, a worldly creature, a study of time, now weeps sitting in his rocking chair, as he counts one painful second after other. I watch him from a corner on days, but don't show myself. Most days, but, I am with Mary, who now lives with my grandmother and me, in our static world, where moments are frozen and no one counts time.

Do you believe in magic? Do you believe in divine intervention? Are you superstitious? Most writers I know are. It would be hard to do what we do without these beliefs. Without having a particular pen that is just for writing in our journals. Without having a journal that only carries the weight of our personal tragedies. How do we do what we do without believing that the world runs on magic? I was never going to be a writer; a string of good and bad decisions led me to what I believe is my purpose on this planet. Is there an explanation for this? Yes, there is. I was always a decent writer. I always did well in the language subjects in school. But poetry?

This poem, *Schizophrenia*, part of a set of three, was written under a spell. I have no other way of describing it. One warm Sunday afternoon, I was lying on the bed in my Delhi home. I did not have a cooler or an air conditioner then. I was too poor for that kind of luxury, or so I would tell myself. I was crying and reminiscing about the good times I had spent with the friend who became a lover and then, by the end of it all was nothing, nor a lover neither a friend. I suddenly got up and started writing. I didn't know where the words were coming from. I didn't know who was writing them for me. It felt like someone inside my body was dictating and I was just the note-taker. One after the other, I wrote and kept writing. My first set of poems.

Before I wrote these three poems I had written no poetry. In fact, the only poetry I had read till then was mandatory school reading. Of course, there were those childish rhyming poems prompted by heartbreak.

Without you there is only pain,
Come back love, I am going insane.

In all fairness to my teenage self, these were just for my diary. I had no intention of showing my scribblings to anyone. What I wrote now, in an almost fevered delirium, was different. No longer was I addressing my heartbreak through poetry. This time, my heartbreak was writing itself. There was a larger purpose to it—my body, tired of carrying all my secrets, was beginning to throw up whatever I was holding inside it. My writing was unshackling me.

The first phase was automatic writing. I would wake up with the urgency of a hungry child desperate for milk. And I would vomit out whatever was inside me. I don't know if you believe in this form of writing, but I do. I've always held that there was something beyond my understanding that brought me to writing. Maybe it was my dead ancestors who wanted me to tell their stories, but I highly doubt it. I think it was the spirit of the dead childhood inside me, raging to be let out in the world and guiding me towards my destiny.

When I started, there were some very clear motifs in my writing. I wrote exclusively about death and the dead. There were spirits in my writing. And there was my grandmother. There was no real reason why I should obsessively write about her. I was not close to my grandmothers, neither of them. I didn't miss them. I didn't love them. I didn't hate them. How could ambivalence prompt a constant presence? It was always my paternal grandmother who would figure in my writings; I knew that. Every time a poem fell out of me and I visualised it, I would see my Aaji in it.

My sudden output could have been a by-product of all the reading I was doing to get over Aditya. I kept myself busy with work and books, and disallowed any feelings of sadness. There were too many writers buzzing in my head at all times. Plath's *The Bell Jar* was the voice of my subconscious. She had taken me to the corners of my mind I didn't know existed.

'I took a deep breath and listened to the old brag of my heart,' said Plath. And like her heart, mine too came back with a resounding pronouncement of, 'I am, I am, I am.' This was a time carved out just for me. Aditya and I were never going to be together. As painful as that was, I had to be honest to myself that I had always known this was how it would be. I could never, in all the time I was in love with him, imagine a future with him. I was not physically attracted to him. I was not excited about our life together. It was his sadness that had drawn me to him. The sadness that led me to my hidden sorrows.

In the immediate aftermath of the breakup though, I was angry. I was angry with Aditya and I was feeling bad for myself. All of life's cruelties started coming back to me. Things I had hidden in the deep dark corners of my body were beginning to come out and haunt me, like the ghosts of my writing.

Karenina's Lover

Don't sleep like that, with your book open on your chest. Don't read till very late in that library, it's haunted, my grandmother used to say. She was a woman of many stories; a woman of many beliefs, my grandmother. Her library, she said, was a place where all the characters came to life. If you listened carefully at night, she said, you could hear them talk. She believed that they were conspiring against her. One time, she said, my grandfather left one such book open. Anna Karenina, that lonely, miserable witch, stepped out of the book that night, and took my grandfather away. My grandmother read the book every night, searching for her husband, Karenina's alleged lover. Karenina was the other woman, I wasn't allowed to like her, or go near her. She knows black magic, that evil Russian, she will cast a spell on you, and take you away too, she would say. Karenina was always locked in my grandmother's cupboard. The day my grandmother died, I set her free. That lonely, miserable witch, lies open on my table now, stripped of her covers, her naked arched back faces me. I long to touch her; hungrily, I wait for her to step down from the table and drag me away, too.

My brother, who is often absent in my poetry, was present in these vignettes flowing out of me. Because I had never had a strong association with my Aaji, and because he was always so close to her, in this poem I imagined the narrator to be a man. Aaji would want to shield him from all the evil Russians and from all the evil women in her life—my Aai, me. I believe that the purpose of the automatic writing was to bring me to my grandmother's story, that you have by now read. Aaji would tell me her story whenever she found the time. But I was too busy, too preoccupied in my indifference towards her to string together the meaning of what she was trying to say.

When the ghosts that haunted both of us started forming these poems for me, Aaji's story, too, fell into place. Could it be, then, that it was Aaji's dead daughter, who I imagine would have loved me if she were alive, doing that? Like I said, these poems were coming to me like a spell, I almost wasn't the one writing them. I was just the pen, the ink, the vessel holding these poems, these stories. Maybe my dead Aatya, Aaji's daughter, was the spirit spelling out magic for me. Maybe it was her way of asking me to find empathy and forgiveness for her mother, my Aaji? Maybe that is why I was always writing about Aaji.

The process of my writing may have started with Aditya, but he was soon forgotten. He was not really important. The real reason, the only reason he came into my life was so that I could arrive at the doorsteps of poetry. And for that I will always be grateful. Had he not deserted me, my misery would have taken a new shape. And who knows if I would have written poetry then.

After I was done with *The Bell Jar*, I read Helen Oyeyemi's *Mr Fox*, and immediately fell in love with her and the character she created as if just for me—Mary. Mary would go on to define the next phase of my writing. Mary, the schizophrenic vision of Mr Fox, the eponymous character of Oyeyemi's novel, would become my muse, my schizophrenic vision. Plath may have helped me understand myself, she may have nudged me to write my journal chronicling my mental health journey, but the words of my first three poems were handed to me by Oyeyemi. The voice I was writing in wasn't mine, it was hers. This voice would keep changing. From Oyeyemi it would go to Juan Rulfo, and from there it would go to Gabriel Garcia Marquez. Only then would I finally find it. My voice travelled across continents, it kept growing and transforming until it finally came to me.

Oyeyemi's Mary would often sneak into Mr Fox's room and talk to him, mock him, be angry with him and make love to him. My Mary would often come to me, gently caress my forehead and sit on the windowsill of my entirely white room and look at me lovingly. It was how I imagined her. I never saw her of course, she was only a function of my imagination. But I did feel her presence. One night, in Delhi, I was sleeping in my bed. It was a warm summer night. The fan was running at full speed. The street light filtered in through my bedroom window that had no curtains. I felt a hand touch me. At first, I thought it was Avi, back from work, trying to wake me up. I didn't open my eyes, mumbling that I wanted to sleep, and fell right back into deep slumber when the hand caressed me again. This time I opened my eyes. I switched on the lights, checked the other rooms and the bathroom. Avi wasn't home, no one was. Then who could it have been?

It was Mary.

Aaji, the sadist that she was, liked narrating horror stories to me. Growing up on a strong dose of the supernatural, I have always been more than inclined to believe that spirits exist, rather co-exist, with us. Aaji used to think that her daughter died because someone wanted her dead. Someone took away her daughter because she was too beautiful, and that someone was jealous. So they performed black magic and killed her. It is a story I believed. Aaji used to tell me not to wear perfume or shampoo. It attracts the spirits, she'd say. She had many stories. I believed them all.

So when this hand caressed me, it was easy for me to believe it was a spirit, and a benign one at that. For a more rational mind, there would be a different explanation—it was the breeze from my open window, they might say—but I named it Mary and started making up stories about her. My first short story was written about her. I called it 'Storyteller of Augustine.' It is another thing that the story was a complete rip-off of one of Oyeyemi's stories from *Mr Fox*.

When I sent the story out for publishing, it was immediately accepted. Why would it not? It lacked originality, but it was written dreamily. The editor called it Marquez-esque, *One Hundred Years of Solitude* no less. I let him do that. I am not much of a fiction writer and it is something I would soon realise, but in this phase, Mary, who was the storyteller of a fictional village called Augustine, was me.

When Aditya walked out of my life, I suddenly had too many hours to myself. I had spent a good chunk of my time, thinking about him and being there for him. Now, I was free. I had no one to talk to, but also no one to take care of. I had a job, but that was easy. Aditya's exit had started a cycle of self-pity and sadness in me. I was so angry I started talking about how much I deserved love after all I had done for him, to whoever would listen. I remembered this one occasion when I had gone to meet a psychiatrist for Aditya because he was drinking himself insane. I told the doctor all I knew about his life and she, in turn, told me about all I could do to help him in my capacity. Then she asked me why I was doing this. Why was I seeking out a therapist for someone else who wasn't even in the country? And why was I doing therapy for him? It wasn't the most traditional thing to do, she said. I was in love, I told her, but she didn't seem convinced.

This need to make others happy, this compulsion to care for others beyond 'normal' boundaries is usually a response to trauma, she said. I wanted to run away from her. Why are you trying to make your lover happy when you know that he is grieving and will take his time to heal, no matter what, she said. I felt attacked. I just wanted Aditya to be happy. I was young and delusional, of course, but I also knew that if I lost a parent there was no way I would suddenly get over it because I fell in love. However, I didn't want to let go of the idea that my love, and not love in general, could heal him. A relationship, she said, in the face of grief and trauma is impossibly hard. He isn't incapable of loving right now. It would be better if he didn't love anyone, for it would not work out. And while we are on the subject of trauma and love, what is it that you are trying to cure?

I left the psychiatrist's office feeling strangely unsettled. My friends who knew how much I was doing for Aditya were very proud of me. I told them what the psychiatrist said to me about him and it made sense to them, but I didn't tell them about the uncomfortable questions she had raised for me. Aditya didn't know about what I had done. He hadn't asked me to do anything for him, but I had a burning desire to be acknowledged for my efforts anyway. It fell flat on my face when he found out and was angry that I thought he was mad, needed psychiatric help, and that I had told his ex about it, which pushed her further away from him. When he accused me of ruining his life more, I felt rejected, misunderstood, angry.

The doctor's words came back to me—trauma and love don't work well. I was dealing with the post effects of trauma. I just did not know it yet. But his reaction, the aftermath of my visit to the therapist, had pushed me towards the edge. I was tired of being rejected. I did not understand the extent of the sorrow I felt, and found distractions for it. But each distraction unwittingly brought me closer to myself. I had already started writing. I was reading copious amounts of literature. The journey towards self-realisation had started because I wanted to get over a lover.

When I think back, I don't imagine I ever loved Aditya. Loved him as a friend, but never as a lover. He was there in my life so I could pretend to save him while I saved myself. It seems obvious now, but it took a long time for that realisation to strike. A year later I would fall in love with Avi. I would see several therapists. I would develop good and bad coping mechanisms. I would go through intense phases of depression where I would do nothing but just sit and cry or look at walls, imagining patterns on them. I would refuse to step out of the house. I would self-harm. I would go through hell and come back. All so I could tell this story. All so I could become the storyteller of Jabalpur.

I think this is why writing happened to me. I never wanted to become a writer but I became one only so that another story of trauma does not get lost, so that through my story

I can tell the stories of all the children who suffered the way I did, or worse.

After I was done with Helen Oyeyemi's *Mr Fox*, I picked up Juan Rulfo's *Pedro Páramo*. For the uninitiated, *Pedro Páramo* takes place in the fictional village of Comala, which is a ghost town populated by the dead. The night I finished reading the novella I slept restlessly. I went through several episodes of sleep paralysis and woke up early in the morning with a burning desire to write something. There was something itching to come out. I picked up my notebook and started scribbling furiously.

Lolita

MARY is dead. Mary IS dead. Mary is DEAD.

I killed Mary. She's dead.

Mary was a plain looking woman.

She tied her hair in a bun, always.

Even on the day she died.

Mary and I were lovers. We met in a queue.

It feels like yesterday. And she's dead today.

A movie, I have no memory of, we watched as strangers.

She wore a yellow dress, and that bun.

She was a plain looking woman.

Mary loved her lipsticks.

Red was her favourite.

Her Yellow dress and Red lipstick.

134 Red lipsticks. She carried them in her bag.

Even on the day she died.

Drug overdose, says the doctor. She died of it.

Her teeth and her face, both Red.

Cold, as she lay on our bed. Where we made love.

We met in those book cafes,

Those places where pretention marries intellect.

We sat there. I, listening to others. She, reading Nabokov.

I called her Lolita, sometimes.

Sometimes Lo. Lee. Ta.

She's dead now. Lipstick smeared across her face.

Drug overdose. She ate all her lipsticks.

134 Red lipsticks.

She was a girl with an appetite.

The cycle of depression that Aditya had unknowingly set in motion would soon transform into another thing. Mary would eventually die in my imagination. She would stop visiting me. She wouldn't be replaced by anyone else though. I would just stop thinking about her. Avi would replace Aditya in a more permanent way. This time, love would find reciprocation and, just for a little while, my depression would feel absent. Like it had never been there.

Love cannot cure depression, but I was naïve enough to assume that it can. I was still in denial about my depression because Avi's presence was making me feel giddy. I was smiling all the time, my serotonin levels probably off the charts. My stomach was buzzing with happy butterflies instead of the anxious ones. For almost a year, I was too busy making merry to worry about anything. Even if there were fights, and there were big ones, I wouldn't let them get to me. After all, who doesn't quarrel in love?

But depression hadn't vacated the house. It was sitting in a corner, waiting patiently for its turn. And its turn would come soon enough. Avi was the first person I had told about how I was violated as a child. That made him my first confidant. He never probed or asked for details. Sometimes I would want to share them and he would listen carefully, offering no remarks. It was one of his qualities, and it was a quiet relief that I was able to tell someone something so traumatic and not see them outraged or feeling sorry for me. It made me love him more fiercely.

As love bloomed in life, for a little while, sadness withered away. I was doing well in my job, appreciated by my bosses and colleagues. I had found someone I thought I'd be spending the rest of my life with, and I was reading a lot and writing a lot. I had love, life, literature. Pardon my cheesy alliterations, if you can.

If Aditya's exit made me throw myself into reading books that helped me understand myself, Avi's love encouraged me to write. After I opened up about the abuse to Avi, I began craving conversations about it, though I wasn't entirely brave yet. I didn't know if I could claim the attention of others with my sorrows. There were things that were eating me from the inside that I wanted to share with the world but I didn't know how.

So, I started writing about it in covert ways. Every poem I wrote was about it. If I wrote about the Bhopal Gas Tragedy, it was still my tragedy that I was ultimately writing about. In a poem entitled *Dental Hygiene is Very Important*, I began exploring my tragedy with a catastrophic event that took place before I was born, and ended it with the one I survived.

Dental hygiene is very important
Baba once told me about a man
who he was friends with in the 80s.
He lost all his teeth, Baba said,
in the Bhopal Gas Tragedy.
They just fell, the minute gas entered
his room through a half open window.
Just like that, all his teeth, anywhere between 28 and 32,
were on the floor, Aai kept repeating in disbelief.

My flatmate once fell face down
and chipped his front tooth
because there was someone at the door.
My Baba has a half broken tooth too.
A mad buffalo hit him from behind
and he also fell face down.
Now, I don't remember him from the time when his teeth
were whole

Aaji who brushed her teeth
behind locked doors
had fake teeth Baba got made on discount.
Each morning she locked the bathroom

removed her teeth, and scrubbed them clean
before wearing them on.
The one time she forgot to lock the door
I walked in and witnessed the purging;
I have to admit, she looked cute toothless.

A lot of my nightmares are teeth centered.
The man who I kicked hard at his funeral
had tobacco stained teeth
I dream that he offers me a chocolate
and says I should be late, before eating it.
For a seven year old I am clever,
I know he means the Hindi word *late*
How could I not be a writer?
I get puns like no one else.

I often dream of his teeth touching
My milk teeth,
and they fall, all at the same time.
Like the uncle who lost his teeth in Bhopal
I lose mine on the first floor of my friend's house.
The tragedy keeps repeating itself

My teeth have grown back
but they have yellow stains
my dentist blames the chlorine in our water,
he recommends a toothpaste
nine out of ten dentists are sure to recommend.

But here's the thing:
what Aaji was purging that day was an unwanted sighting
and yes, she really did look cute toothless.

It didn't matter what sadness I was writing about, I was always at the centre of it. In the poem *Lolita*, the mother of all obvious metaphors, I was Lolita. I was trying to bring the inner child back to life. The child who had grown up a little too soon. When I sent these poems to people, a lot of the times they liked what they read but understood little. But sometimes, someone would write back asking me about whatever I was trying to hide, and at the same time show, through these poems. And it would scare me but also validate me.

My sadness was out there in the world. If I kept writing about it long enough, others would absorb it and my own sadness would dissolve, little by little. At least that was my hope. Sometimes that did happen. But the more I wrote, the more people read and understood, and the more questions they came back with. All these memories I had kept hidden started surfacing. I had no option other than to face them. I often wonder what if I had continued to keep it all in? For one, I would not be a writer and maybe that would not have been such a bad thing. But now that we are already in the thick of things, might as well have some fun with it.

When I think about all the writing I did in that phase of life, it almost feels prophetic. Some of the poems predated some events in my life. I wrote poems about love that was falling through the cracks of the walls of our house and slowly dissipating. Was I writing about my own love and the relationship I shared with Avi?

Writing saved me. It has always saved me. I would write about mosquitoes that I swatted and that had died leaving a bloody imprint on the wall. I would write about our oily scalps leaving imprints of our sadness on that wall. That wall was a metaphor for that messy space in my head that desperately needed cleaning but was always overlooked. When the happy sheen of new love wore off, I was again left with my books and my writing. Love should exist beyond the highs and lows. I don't want to demean my love and my former lover, but for me it did run out. I was too sick, too sad, too broken to keep myself content with what we had. I needed to be put together first. But Avi had his own problems. When our depressions began clashing with each other I retreated inwards. I developed bad coping mechanisms. But kept reading and writing.

Like a grown up Matilda I read and read and read. And I wrote. Isn't this why I am writing this book anyway, because I am hoping it will save me? It has taken a lot of time and hard work to reach a point where I can just write and not return to my terrible coping mechanisms. Not hurt myself. Not overeat or undereat. Not just sleep or be up all night doing nothing. It can come at a grave cost. It has not been easy. It never is.

PART IV

1

'I cannot make you understand. I cannot make anyone understand what is happening inside me. I cannot even explain it to myself.'

—Franz Kafka, *The Metamorphosis*

ONCE UPON A TIME I loved a boy and he loved me too. In Delhi, during autumn—the season of love and longing, or sadness and departures—our love blossomed. We were madly in love until we weren't or I wasn't. The love that warmed us in the harsh Delhi winters, that was as permanent as the dried flowers found in old books, was supposed to live forever. But forever, like the White Rabbit told Alice when she asked, lasts for, 'sometimes, just one second.'

Avi and I got our second. It lasted a few summers, and then it was gone. One day we were floating in the clouds, giddy with love, the next day gravity got the better of us and pushed us to the ground. We fell but in slow motion. What happened to us, and when did this fall begin?

When Avi and I fell into the habit of being in love, we started taking advantage of each other. I had only started unpacking my traumas. I had just found a therapist and was speaking about the years of abuse I had lived through, for the first time. At last my pain had found a voice, but that wasn't all. My self-awareness came with a set of traits that would require an understanding, I still hadn't developed. How could I expect someone else to get it, when I was grappling with it too?

When Avi and I hit a rough patch in our relationship, I turned quiet. It wasn't that I wouldn't fight at all, I would, but I would also swallow words and anger and act out sometimes with passive aggression. I was quick to apologise. I was quick to 'forgive', but not really. I would have all my fights inside my head. I was not at peace. I was afraid, afraid that I would hurt him.

For the longest time I assumed that the reason I could not speak up for myself was that I had a great amount of empathy. If I lashed out I would hurt Avi and cause too much damage. He didn't deserve that. Truthfully, it helped me continue to feel sorry for myself. I could throw as many pity-parties as I liked if I was the silent, suffering partner in an emotionally abusive relationship. And it was an emotionally abusive relationship.

I do believe that I was silenced, perhaps unintentionally. Without meaning to, Avi placed his traumas over mine. I think what helped his cause was that I was a people pleaser, but it wasn't just that. It was what would happen when I confronted the conflict. People would get hurt, and that would make them like me less. I could not handle that. A pretty common trait in people who have grown up in abusive surroundings.

When the childhood abuse stopped abruptly, I was left wondering what had happened. What had I done? Why did no one love me anymore? I was scared that I might have done something wrong. The abandonment, because that is how I saw it, was agony.

What if I talked to them, what if I went to their house, what if I dressed provocatively? How does one dress provocatively? When it all started, no one took my permission. When it stopped no one talked to me about it. It was abandonment and I couldn't understand it. I carried the scars within me.

When the conflict with Avi began there were small incidents of him putting too much pressure on me, of him relying too much on me, of him walking out mid-fights, of him taking out his aggression on me through cruel words. These incidents kept accumulating. Relationship rituals, like picking each other up from the airport, started feeling like a burden to me. When it was new it was great. But neither of us had a car. Neither of us were madly in love. Neither of us needed to spend money on picking the other up two years after being comfortably in love.

Perhaps I should have made more effort, but it had started to feel as if he was demanding these things of me. In the middle of my depressive episodes, when leaving the bed was hard enough, he wanted me to travel all the way to the airport to receive him. When at one point I told him I didn't want to do it, he responded with, 'But I always come to pick you up!' He did. But I didn't want him to; I wasn't making him. I should have said it, but didn't. The burden of his decision was on me.

Every time I held back my responses I was trying to placate him because dealing with his anger felt scarier. Every time I held back my responses I was letting down the child in me who couldn't stand up for herself.

The biggest blow to our relationship and my self-esteem came a few months later, when Avi cheated on me in our house, in my presence. A friend, I'll call her P, had come to stay with us for a couple of days. There was a water problem in her hostel. We cooked good food for her and watched a film that night. After the film we were talking, when I realised that I was beginning to drift off to sleep. Eventually, I could stay up no longer and went to bed while Avi and P moved to the living room to continue talking. I woke up around 6 a.m. to a quiet house and a gnawing feeling in my gut that something was wrong.

I got up and, without making any noise, peeped into the adjoining room and saw what I didn't want to see. My entire body burned with anxiety. I tried to calm down. I tried to fall back to sleep. I wanted to pretend like nothing had happened. A part of me wanted to see how far Avi would take it. But it was all too much and I couldn't contain myself. I sent three messages to a friend.

'I just saw Avi making out with P.'

'What am I supposed to do?'

'I don't know what is happening but I think I will throw up.'

I got up to go to the washroom, crossing the both of them who were now aware that I had seen them. P smiled at me awkwardly and I broke into loud tears. I almost ran inside the bathroom, shut the door behind me and splashed a lot of water on my face. I then went back to the bedroom, avoiding the two other people in the house. As I attempted to close the door Avi tried to push his way in. Eventually, I let him inside, but there was no conversation to be had in that moment. I was not prepared for rage, nor was I prepared for forgiveness. I texted Navni and she came to pick me up. And I left the house.

When I finally returned after three days, and tried to have a conversation with him, Avi immediately made me regret it. He apologised. When I asked him what would have happened had I not seen the two of them, he said he wouldn't have told me. It meant nothing to him, he said. And then he tried to pin it on me, saying I had kept myself away from him and he had not felt any love for a while, which is what led to his infidelity. He offered many apologies but each one of them felt conditional.

I was hurt, but the truth is that I had been hurting for a while. He had presented me with an opportunity to break free from him, I only had to grab it. But instead I forgave him. Not only was I not ready to give up on our relationship, I was also not willing to hurt him despite what he had done.

It was an extremely puzzling period. No one understood why I could not end things. I didn't understand it either. After all these years of reliving the trauma of his infidelity, I finally know why it was so hard for me to let go. Simply put, I don't want to be hated. Cutting someone out of my life would necessitate a harshness that would lead to the other person disliking me. I can't stand that. It has taken me a lot of time to realise that what I thought was empathy was actually my PTSD talking.

I was raped inside my own house, where my grandmother disowned me by not helping me out, by abandoning me when I needed her the most. Avi cheating on me in my house, a space that I thought was safe, felt like a repeat of that incident. A doubling of that trauma. I started experiencing flashbacks. I couldn't enjoy intimacy. Everything reminded me of the childhood abuse. I didn't like him touching me. I didn't like him wanting me. I just wanted to be left alone. But I also couldn't let him go.

I was also experiencing massive health anxiety. It had been a year since I had been hospitalised because of the Rotavirus infection. The visit had left me shaken. I was constantly scared of catching another stomach bug. That fear grew to accomodate bigger anxieties of cancer, heart attack, liver failure, everything. I was so consumed by this outstanding and all round grief that I was constantly exhausted. I had stopped feeling desire and had given up on sex. I was overeating and then undereating. I was unhealthy. I just wanted to be numb. And I stumbled upon that numbness by accident.

I have always had hormonal imbalance issues; I have been on medication for thyroid since puberty. I have always had facial hair and been made to feel conscious about it. In the middle of this emotionally chaotic phase I was home in Jabalpur visiting my parents. While getting ready for some excursion, I found Aai's old tweezers. I was beginning to notice some hair growth on my chin and since I don't enjoy parlour visits, I thought I would tweeze them out.

The tweezers were too old and misshapen to work, so my facial hair remained intact. But later that evening when Aai and I were shopping for some make up, I asked her to buy a pair of tweezers and she did. I wish she hadn't.

When we returned home, I stood in front of the mirror and carefully plucked out one chin hair. In that moment, in front of the mirror, I could see myself transform into something I couldn't quite understand. There was this momentary relief that I felt travel through my anxiety-ridden body. The slight pain I had felt when I pulled that hair, was so enjoyable that I immediately craved it. Instinctively my hand went back to my chin and I plucked out another strand.

I didn't just throw what I was plucking out either. I was so taken by this entire process and how it made me feel that I started gathering them, observing their roots, awestruck. It was only after I had collected the hairs I had pulled out, and admired them, did I discard them.

That first night, when I started plucking the hair, I spent more than five hours doing it. I was up until four in the morning doing nothing but pulling my hair, from my chin, from the upper neck region, from my forehead, my legs, and arms, I pulled out everything unwanted. It was the first time in months that I hadn't thought about falling ill, or how much I wanted to leave Avi. It was the first time in months that I was feeling nothing but plain relief from that gut wrenching pain I carried within my body. So what if I had to inflict a different kind of pain on myself for that?

When I started pulling out my hair I didn't know it was going to become an obsession. I was just trying to get rid of the hideousness growing on my body. I grew up listening to my parents, relatives and neighbours telling me how fat I was and how I had to lose weight to look good, to find a boyfriend, to be healthy. Not so much my Baba, who just wanted me to not be out of breath each time I climbed a hillock or a flight of stairs, but the others could not separate my body fat from who I was.

The body fat, of course, was responsible for the hormone imbalance while also being caused by it. I was fat because of genetic reasons. Aai, too, had hormonal imbalances, Aai, too, was fat when she was young. I was no different. But because I didn't do anything about my fat, my hormones never settled. My periods were often late, sometimes arriving once in two months. I had developed cysts in my uterus. I had hypothyroidism. And a product of all these was facial hair.

If I hadn't been raped, I wouldn't be fat. If I hadn't been raped, I would have not associated being fat with being ugly. If I hadn't been fat, my hormones would be under control. With my hormones under control, I would not have as much facial hair as I did. If I wasn't constantly told that being fat was ugly, and facial hair on a girl was unsightly, I would not have picked up those tweezers. If I hadn't picked up those tweezers I would not have developed Trichotillomania, for that was what my obsessive fascination with pulling out hair was called.

Trichotillomania is defined as a disorder that involves a recurrent and irresistible urge to pull out body hair. It could be from the scalp, eyebrows, chin … any part of the body. Mental illnesses are invisible disabilities most of the time. If you look at me, most days you won't be able to tell that I have depression or anxiety or PTSD. The marks are hidden, unless you are self-harming and not covering up your scars. But even within invisible disabilities there are some that are more invisible than others. Trichotillomania is one of them.

No one talks about it and very few seem to know about it. After plucking my chin hair obsessively for a month, I finally had to admit to myself that this was not normal. I knew that it was keeping me numb. I knew that it was helping me distract myself. But I also knew that my hands itched to reach for the tweezer, more and more often. It was becoming difficult to stop. I was impossible to hide. I was becoming a freak show. I turned to the internet for answers and Google put a label on my madness.

For me, my hair pulling was a symptom of anxiety. Google said it was also associated with a hint of body dysmorphia, but I wasn't ever diagnosed with it. I was doing it because I hated my facial hair and being without a strand of hair on my chin felt like it would make me look better, or at least acceptable. Aren't we always taught how we are supposed to be hairless? Hair on women except for their scalp is never acceptable. If you have been made fun of because of that beard-like hair, you hate it even more. The sense of relief that the hair pulling was bringing me aside, the reason I specifically went for the hair on my chin was because of the strong social conditioning. The price of beauty is pain, after all.

When I discovered my illness, I didn't know anyone else who had it. Not a single character in popular culture was assigned this unglamorous illness. Some disorders are so invisible that you tend to not pay them attention unless they happen to you.

One day, I was sitting in front of my laptop, tweezers in hand, watching *Grey's Anatomy*. I had seen all these episodes before, but I enjoyed the reruns and watched the show often. Suddenly I spotted a fellow sufferer of my new disease. In the show, a patient who pulled her hair when anxious was diagnosed with it. The next time it was Mitchell in *Modern Family*. And the latest was Adora Crellin played by Patricia Clarkson in *Sharp Objects*.

The great thing about pop-culture representation is that it makes you feel tremendously less lonely. I have what she has is a great way of explaining your tragedies to those who don't understand. I remember feeling this rush of happiness when I saw that *Grey's Anatomy* episode. I felt grateful as I plucked out another hair and placed it neatly in front of me.

Trichotillomania gave me a new kind of high. With each hair I pulled, I would feel relief spread all over my body. It would go away the second I stopped. Which is why I never stopped, I kept tugging at my chin. I kept pulling out every single strand of hair. Sometimes I would get so deeply absorbed in it that I would forget the world around me. I would forget that I was suffering, that I was afraid of dying, of falling ill. That I had a relationship crumbling in front of my eyes that needed fixing. I'd forget everything. Maybe that was the point.

After spending time with my parents I came back to Delhi. A little different this time, a little more damaged. The hair pulling continued. It had reached such heights that people around me were beginning to get worried. Everyone would yell at me. Everyone but Avi. He never said anything about it. Sometimes I wondered if he even noticed the madness I was subjecting myself to. I assumed it didn't bother him because he never asked me to stop. And I was always grateful for that. At least here, in my house, I could do whatever I wanted to do with my body without being questioned.

Other friends would snatch away the tweezers and hide them. They would yell at me to stop. My obsession had begun leaving its marks—my relentless tweezing under my chin caused dark patches, that looked like a pair of lungs, to appear. I would often end up injuring my skin because, in my frenzy to pull out hair, I would sometimes end up tugging on my naked skin. I would pull the tweezers with such force that small pieces of skin would peel off. And then as scabs would grow I would keep probing the injured areas because the pain felt good.

The pain had become necessary for me. It numbed me when reality got too much to take, and jolted me right back when the numbness got exhausting. The pain would remind me I was alive without overwhelming me. This pain I could understand, I could live with. Instead of fixing my relationship or ending it, instead of taking hard decisions and acting on them, I kept myself busy with the hair pulling. The result of that still rests on my chin.

I was so deeply involved in this exercise of self-harm that I would sleep with tweezers underneath my pillows. If I woke up because of a nightmare I would fumble for the tweezers and start the process of pulling my hair, till I felt calm again. The dark patches that began on my chin had spread to my upper neck area, but it was too late to stop now. I was addicted to the kind of pain the hair pulling gave me.

Probably disgusted by my inability to stop myself, one day a friend hid my tweezers somewhere. I tried to look for them everywhere. I turned the entire house upside down in my desperate search. I took out all the clothes from my cupboard and haphazardly dumped them right back in when I couldn't find the tweezers there. I went through every single bag I had. I even sifted through the garbage bin. I spent two days searching for them, with my hand constantly running over my chin, checking the hair growth, every touch filling me with self-loathing.

When the search yielded nothing, I stepped out of the house, something I wasn't doing much in those days, went to Saket J Block market and bought myself a pair of tweezers. I was in such a mad rush to get back home, I forgot to bargain with the auto guy, overpaid him, rushed up the stairs, fumbled with my keys, opened the door, and plopped myself on the bed with the tweezers in hand. When I pulled one hair anticipating relief, none came. The tweezers were all wrong, they weren't working. I tried and tried again but couldn't pluck a single hair. The build-up of anxiety was so great I started crying. I was wailing in pain, a pain that wasn't physical but psychological. It was an inexplicable pain.

I had made all the effort of stepping out of the house to buy the tweezers and it had all come to naught. I was angry at my friend for putting me through this ordeal. Avi was confused. He didn't understand what was happening but he also knew that I was used to getting into these episodes of exhaustion and dread where I would resort to crying. He tried to comfort me but how could he?

I went and bought a new pair of tweezers later that day and things went back to normal. 'Normal' here, of course, was me in front of my laptop with a floral printed pair of tweezers in one hand, plucking one hair after another.

Scenes at a Dermatology Clinic

The skin is the body's biggest organ, Aai informs me like she used to when she was still my favourite teacher. She once taught me how to spell the word 'thoroughly' and I aced my dictation test. The teacher counted my friends' collective failures on her fingers, and when she ran out of them, she declared, *I am thoroughly surprised that most of you couldn't spell 'thoroughly'.*

You must take care of your skin, Aai declares. I nod in agreement and dial the dermatologist's number. I am given an appointment but I have to wait a month. As I wait, the rot on my skin grows. Ever since I lost my sanity, I cannot breathe without inflating my lungs. Every time I breathe, my lungs leave imprints on my double chin. And now I have dark lung-like patches growing on my skin. My second pair of lungs resembles those of cancer patients in government hospitals. *You are a hopeless case*, says Aai and I concede.

Stop tugging on those hairs. You will rip open your flesh someday, and words will fall off and desert you, she warns me. But I keep tugging. I collect hair like people collect trophies. At the dermatologist's clinic, a little girl is growing warts on her skin. I ask her how she feels about removing them and she looks scared. *Why will I remove them*, she enquires. *I grew them, they belong to me.*

And sadness grows on me. Because I know I get rid of what is mine every day. I chip little parts of me and brush them off. The dermatologist is only going to fill in the cavities I leave behind. He makes me touch his hand, and assures me he will take care of the mess I have created. My skin will be as nourished as his. The little girl with warts stands on the weighing scale. *17 kilos*, shouts the dermatologist. *Warts and all*, I mumble. She looks worriedly in my direction, and says, *Exactly*.

I had written this poem when a friend who edits a journal on sexuality and disabilities called *Skin Stories* asked me to. I had written an essay for them on Trichotillomania and she wanted the poem to accompany the piece. Like much of life, here as well, wisdom came to me through the process of writing. I was doing little else when I was plucking my chin hair. I was occupying myself with nothingness. I was not reading, I was not writing, I was not thinking. I wasn't fighting either. The moments when I wasn't using the tweezers, say while bathing, or meeting a friend outside the house, I was either talking about Avi or having fights with him in my head.

But I couldn't face him so I avoided looking at him entirely. It wasn't fair on him, but I could not bear the thought of hurting him and seeing hatred for me on his face. I needed him to like me; I needed the façade of this to keep working, or I would feel like a failure and that was too much to deal with.

As a kid, when I was abandoned by those men, especially Ajit, it wasn't easy on me but I could not do anything about it. No one asked me anything, I was merely a passive party to the goings-on. Now, my brain that already took abuse for love was trying very hard to finish what had started when I was little. It wanted me to achieve closure by getting to the finish line this time. It wanted me to have a full relationship even if it made me unhappy. I had not been happy as a kid either when the abuse was happening. Why should this be any different? I was so trained to accept sadness and pain in love, that I kept on accepting these things without realising what I was doing. I was angry and resentful but I was also desperate to stay in the relationship, contrary to what I told my friends. How long could this have lasted?

How long could I keep watching *Grey's Anatomy*, deny Avi affection, and still stay in this unhappy relationship? I wanted it to work, but I wasn't willing to fight for it. I wanted him to apologise to me and really mean it. I wanted to fall back in love with him. I wanted to end silences. But instead I was just pulling my hair, chipping away parts of me, and holding on to unfulfilled childhood expectations. Avi, I know, was beginning to see the cracks in our relationship.

I had stopped saying I love you. If he ever said that to me, I would just change the subject to avoid saying it back. It felt dishonest. One evening, Avi in an urgent desire for affection, took me to Dunkin' Donuts. He knew how much I loved donuts and this particular outlet was one of our old haunts. We took a small table and ordered two donuts and two coffees. I was eating, the only thing I was really interested in, when I felt Avi's foot trying to gently rub mine. It came as a rude jolt to me that I didn't feel anything but anger at what he was trying to do. It felt like he was forcing his affection on me, when all he was trying to do was make me feel loved and maybe take us back to where we had started.

But it's not that easy to go back to that place of love when so much has gone wrong. I was constantly having trouble forgetting what I had seen that night when he had strayed. His touch felt like a violation. I withdrew my foot from underneath his and kept eating to stop myself from crying. He tried to hold my hand, so I placed one over the coffee mug, while with the other I tore the donut to pieces. I had known in my heart that I had to end this, but just how irreparable we had become was only apparent to me that evening at Dunkin'. Our love was now tainted. It was as good as over.

2

'After all, my erstwhile dear,
My no longer cherished,
Need we say it was not love,
Just because it perished?'

—Edna St. Vincent Millay

IN 2016, I COMPLETED my MA from Ambedkar University, Delhi. Despite the lengthy periods of depression and anxiety, I had done remarkably well throughout college. My grades were stellar, I was well-liked by students as well as teachers. I had already been in therapy for two years by then and was seeing my fourth therapist by the time college ended. My therapist—I am going to call her Zainab—was the best I had been to so far. She was sharp, focused, well-read, and taught me much about my ticks and behavioural issues.

When I started seeing her, I was already in my second year of college and my second year of obsession with stomach maladies. I had spent all of 2014 worrying myself sick over my stomach related issues. I had lost all sense of what was good for my health and what was not. I had eaten rice all of that year. Whenever I wanted to eat something that was not dal chawal or khichri, I would turn to something sweet. Ice cream could not hurt my stomach I thought, why not eat one medium tub of Baskin-Robbins or London Dairy.

Donuts from Dunkin' were not Chinese food, they were not going to harm me. The Big Chill café made the best cheesecakes, how could that give me any trouble? Eating ice creams and cakes from high-end places was a safe bet. At least I was not eating gol gappas which I loved, but which carried far too many pathogens.

By the time 2015 arrived I had relaxed my strict eating habits a bit, though I was still quite paranoid. I would occasionally eat a cheese sandwich from the kiosk at the university, which was delicious and had excessive amounts of mayo and chipotle sauce. I have this theory that the more unsanitary the thing, the greater its taste value. It is absolutely unscientific, but until the gol gappa guy dips his hands in the tub of spicy gol gappa water, it just doesn't taste right. The sandwich kiosk would definitely not pass any food inspection standards, hence it was delicious and just what all students needed. I, too, would lunch on such delicacies as their cheese sandwich and butter Maggi on some days. On other days I would go without lunch.

I was rapidly putting on weight, but I didn't have much time to worry about that. I had a stomach to obsess over, I had papers to write, I had therapy to attend, a crumbling relationship to mend, panic attacks to have, and friendships to build. It was a busy life. By 2015 I had already left my first therapist. The second one came highly recommended by a friend. He offered me a discounted rate too because of my ties to people close to him.

I am going to call him Dr Nil, because it hides his real identity and rhymes with Dr Phil. My MBBS doctor therapist was someone who did alternate therapy. He was very sweet and chatty. And he liked me. Before Dr Nil, I was seeing a therapist who came with a unique set of challenges. She was kind and had a soft and almost scared voice, and she could not speak one sentence in English without making grammatical mistakes. Sometimes she'd misuse words and change the meaning of whatever she wanted to say. I had empathy for her problems with the English language, but this was therapy. I needed to understand what my therapist was saying without too much effort. Which was just not possible with her.

I would switch to Hindi often in the hope that she'd do the same but she never did. Finally, I gave up. I sat without a therapist for a few months, pulling my chin hair, crying into my pillows, experiencing fits of rage and grave moments of despair, till it all became unbearable again. Desperate, I wrote to a friend who recommended Dr Nil. I started seeing Nil in March 2015, and I continued to see him for the next three months, one session a week. In June when the second semester of MA ended, I left for Jabalpur to spend time with my parents and Nil and I ended our sessions.

The next two months I was feeling better, but the hair pulling continued. I came back to Delhi, end of July, and the third semester started. I had taken interesting subjects this semester, one on European Cinema, and one called Examining Normalcy where we dealt with literature and art that represented the themes of madness through the past centuries. I was really having a good time with the courses. I had made new friends and I loved hanging out with them. I was liked by my professors, and I was talking more openly to anyone willing to listen—friends and compassionate strangers alike—about my struggles with mental illnesses and my past. Despite the fact that Avi and I were no longer in love the way we once used to be, my life was significantly easier and I felt in control. I would have worked on my relationship, now that I was feeling stronger and better, but then Avi cheated on me.

College kept us busy. We were no longer just two people depending on each other most of the time. We had other people, we had friends, we had conversations that were enriching us. But I was still depressed, depression doesn't just vanish. I had my fears. I had my anxieties. I was still preoccupied with them. While I made time for these things, and while I was still present for Avi emotionally, I was not present for him as his lover. I was his friend but maybe not more than that. I felt too fragile to be anything more. And I think Avi did feel that distance though he didn't complain. He had his concerns, he had his emotional baggage, and I was resisting him, unable to hold him. I don't know why Avi didn't say anything. Had he said something maybe things would have been different. Or maybe he did say something and I didn't listen.

On 21 August 2015, Avi crossed a line he should not have. His breathtaking cruelty left me so broken I am still gathering the pieces. The fact that I got a live viewing of his indiscretions took away a lot of my recovery and healing, and I found myself standing in front of the same doors I had pushed open to make my way in. I retreated into therapy again. But I didn't want to go back to Nil, which is why I wrote to the Ehsaas clinic people. My professor, whose sister was the head of the psychology department at Ambedkar University, got me a quick appointment because I had begun self-harming and was contemplating suicide.

My new therapist, Dr Rakesh, knew English but was not a very good listener, or if he was, he didn't understand what was happening to me. I spent several sessions trying to explain all my problems and he would come up with cookie cutter responses. I desperately needed someone to talk to, so I continued with him for a few sessions. I needed someone to help me, someone to hear me out. Even if he wasn't very helpful, at least he was there, and eager to help me. At least I had a therapist. Maybe, if I tried very hard to explain my situation to him, he would say something meaningful? I was quite used to blaming myself for any failures, perceived or real. So, maybe I wasn't trying hard enough, I thought.

But a bad therapist is almost always worse than no therapist. A bad therapist can consciously, or subconsciously change or worsen your perception about yourself. Therapists can gaslight. Bad therapists can be unkind, cruel, or just plain unhelpful. And if it is hard to get yourself to a therapist's office, it is harder still to leave the office of a bad therapist without any invisible scars. It is why many tend to latch on to bad therapists, it is why many end up believing everything their therapists say.

My poor listener therapist was reinforcing, in subtle ways, the idea that I am not worth listening to. That it was okay to not pay attention to my problems. I would often doubt the veracity of my illnesses and my therapist not hearing me out properly made me feel dismissed, kept reinforcing the idea that the voices in my head were right—I didn't have anything.

When Avi cheated on me it had a profound impact on me. He had been my support system for so long that I was extremely dependent on his presence, but I couldn't trust him anymore. I couldn't leave him, and now I couldn't be with him. I was stuck in a limbo. The day he cheated on me, Navni came and took me to eat something. I couldn't eat, but I smoked seven cigarettes one after the other, and had a very public meltdown at SDA market, where I sat on the filthy floor outside Chaayos, and cried my lungs out.

My self-esteem had hit a new low. You don't want to be the girl who gets cheated on. And you definitely don't want to be the girl who gets cheated on in her own house, while she is in the next room. I had felt invisible all my life, but this level of invisibility, where I was forgotten by the man I loved so completely that he didn't acknowledge my presence merely ten metres away, was something I hadn't anticipated.

I remember that when the cheating episode happened we were to watch *Hiroshima Mon Amour* in my European Cinema class. I watched the film and made notes, pushing away my personal crises, but it was not easy.

In the film, the female protagonist played by French actress Emmanuelle Riva, comes to Japan on a film shoot. She meets the (might I add) fantastically attractive Japanese actor Eiji Okada and they begin a thirty-six hour long affair. Through the course of the film, we see them talk about the Second World War and its impact on the characters, and of course the Hiroshima bombing. We see Riva compare the bombing and the wreckage it left behind to her failed relationships.

As I was watching Riva relive the traumatic memories of her past and come to terms with the fact that she must again leave her new lover behind and go back to her old life, I kept thinking how this was a doubling of her trauma. After living through a round of assault, she is experiencing the same thing again. And suddenly I knew that Avi cheating on me in my own house, in front of my eyes, had affected me so terribly because it had doubled my trauma. Yet again, someone I trusted had violated my safe space.

The next day, armed with this profound realisation, I went and poured my heart out to Dr Rakesh, this time sure that I had something concrete to talk about. After I had narrated the story of *Hiroshima Mon Amour*, and how my own life ran parallel to it, he paused and with a pained expression he asked me, 'So, you now feel like you were in the Hiroshima bombing?' It was a great tragi-comic moment. I didn't know if I should continue crying or take a break from that and laugh. This was my life—a boyfriend who cheats and a therapist who does not understand what I say.

I discontinued therapy with the man after that, but I also knew I needed a new therapist. Going back to Nil was out of the question. There were several reasons for that, the foremost being that he was now treating Avi. The other equally important reason was that I was slowly but surely realising that Nil's behaviour towards me as a therapist had not been completely ethical. He had breached a lot of codes of doctor-patient boundaries.

The relationship a patient shares with their therapist is as precarious as it is complicated. There's a person who knows you inside out, who you talk to about everything, no matter how difficult, no matter how dark, but get no judgment in return, only understanding and compassion. I have wanted to befriend all my therapists, I have felt a twinge of jealousy that they have other friends and partners, other people who are important to them. I remember an incident, when I heard someone talk about my therapist. I felt an excitement within me—someone I knew so closely was being discussed. I would have stories to share as well. Only, I didn't. I didn't really know my therapist despite the intimate relationship we shared. And that is exactly what made them a good therapist.

Not Nil though. Nil didn't just give me the illusion of friendship, he actually offered me that. I was new to the concept of therapy in those days. I felt wonderful that my therapist found me so interesting that he wanted to be my friend. I knew about his family, his experiences back home, his struggles with his partner. My therapist told me he'd like to be my friend once therapy was over, should I agree to it. My therapist gave me agency. It was too easy to get sucked into that hole of desire. But it was not right. It never is right.

His alternate therapy methods didn't work for me, but I don't blame him for that. I lacked faith in their effectiveness and could never open up my mind enough to accept them. And yet, I had also met him at such a desperate phase in my life, that no matter how much I doubted the science behind his methods, I kept going back to him. I would try to find answers in whatever he said and made me do. I was dishonest with myself and I have no one to blame for that.

But what Nil also did was try to befriend me. He took away the impartiality that a therapist's couch must guarantee. We would often end up discussing the people we knew in common. Even though we weren't really friends during the therapy sessions I knew about his partner. He would send me his works for feedback and would want my help in literary projects. He even indulged me when I'd want to bitch about people by adding to my stories. The boundaries of friendship and his role in my life as a therapist were often breached during therapy.

So far, I have had five therapists and no one other than Nil has ever given me that kind of access to their personal life. My therapist trusted me so much he told me about his family, his partner, their fights, the guests they would have over. The fact that a lot of these conversations happened while I was in the middle of therapy with him, gave me a false sense of safety. It also made me feel immensely proud of myself. None of my friends had such a relationship with their therapist.

I had opened my heart to Nil, like one is supposed to in therapy, and it meant that I was too vulnerable to understand that what was happening was damaging. When the therapy sessions ended for good, Nil invited me to his place. We had a glass of wine, smoked a joint, and he asked me if I'd like to be his friend. He told me I could cut him out of my life entirely and not acknowledge his presence if I preferred. But the truth was we had already become friends before these rules were explained to me. How could I say no, then?

I understood the full extent of his influence on me when I went to him, after the Dr Rakesh fiasco, to ask him for a recommendation for a new therapist. Now that we were friends officially, I would not want him to go back to being my therapist, but as a friend I could cry about Avi to him. Of course, it was a complicated situation since Avi was his client. What made things worse was he tried to gaslight me by telling me how apologetic Avi was about what he had done. It was not Avi's fault, the girl had come on to him, he added.

As if that wasn't enough, he delegitimised my rage by insisting that I was being harsh on Avi. I had had enough. I didn't say anything, but decided to distance myself from Nil. A few months later I got a call from Nil to inform me that he and his partner had split and he had moved in to a new house that I had to check out. That's what friends do, right?

They inform each other about everything that happens in their lives. At that time I was contemplating moving out of the house I shared with Avi. On hearing that, Nil asked me if I'd like to move in with him. He made it sound like it was the most natural thing to do. We were friends, we could live together, couldn't we?

The thought of living with my ex therapist and current friend was strange yet comforting. Who better to help you during your episodes of crippling panic attacks than a friend who knows every detail about you and is also a trained therapist? When I told my friends about Nil's proposal they warned me against the idea. There should be some boundaries, they said. I didn't end up moving in with Nil, but it was an unsettling thought that stuck in my head, that my friends understood therapist-patient boundaries better than the man who had the training to be a therapist.

My unorthodox relationship with my therapist should have been punishable by law. But we are a country where people don't want to talk about mental illnesses, where depression is just sadness, everything else is madness, and mad folk are found wandering on the roads, covered in dirty rags throwing stones at other 'normal' people. If we don't even like talking about it, there is no way our politicians are ever going to take out the time to write a bill, and pass laws. We are all functioning on good faith or not functioning at all. If you get romantically involved with a therapist, there might be emotional consequences for you, but there won't be any legal ones for the therapist. In the absence of any laws penalising these actions, patients are in an extremely vulnerable space. It is, then, the moral and ethical responsibility of the therapist to ensure a professional and safe environment for their patients.

Nil and I were never in a romantic space; that's not what this is about. He had too much power over me; the scales were dangerously tipped in his favour. The role I had assigned him was of someone who would help me heal. He had no business using that role to gain influence on me and then try to shift how we related to each other. I had gone to seek help but once again I was in the same spot. Yet another man was violating my personal space, putting his needs above mine. Yet again, I did not know what to do or how to remedy the situation other than to move away.

He did recommend someone to me, and just for that I can forgive his many wrongdoings. Zainab, the therapist he sent me to is the best I have seen to this day. I can't imagine the last three years without her.

I don't know about others, but for me, my therapy learning has always come in the form of action first, reflection later. While Nil and I extensively discussed my health anxiety, my relationship with Avi and the crippling fear I often felt about the mortality of my parents, I could never really get any answers. This was not Nil's fault, I was always a bit sceptical of his methods and never fully committed to them. But I still needed help.

I needed more conversations, a more analytical examination. In Zainab, I found what I was looking for. It helped that she was well read and understood my literary references. She was also extremely sharp and posed challenging questions that made me think hard, and come up with answers to my problems. When I couldn't, she would point me towards them, but make me do the intellectual labour.

In the first few sessions, I obsessively talked about my stomach related phobias. I had read enough on the internet to know that stomach troubles are often associated with anxiety. The internet couldn't tell me why the Rotavirus attack felt so traumatic, though. It wasn't my first serious food poisoning episode. It wasn't even my first stay at the hospital. So, what could explain it?

When I asked Zainab, she asked me a series of questions about my child sexual abuse experiences. When did I start talking about it? Who did I open up to? How long had it been? How many people now knew about this? I answered her diligently. Some four years back, in 2012, I had told Avi. He was the first person to know. And most of my close friends knew about it now. She asked me to think about the stress of a relationship that had stopped making me feel good. How did it make me feel?

How was I coping with the loss of a relationship the way I had imagined it to be, and how was I dealing with the loss of faith in my confidant? What were my fears? What were my experiences? I again attempted to address her, and slowly the answer to my own dilemma revealed itself. Was my stomach upset not only a subset of my anxiety but also a physical manifestation of trauma and all the pain it brought along?

Zainab's office was in the basement of someone's house

in Alaknanda colony. The room would be cool and dark, I suppose to foster a sense of comfort, but there was always enough light to see her reassuring smile. She always lit some candles in the room which had a big couch along with a comfortable chair. For the first few sessions, I sat on the chair. Once we hit the realisation that it wasn't the Rotavirus, but my body's reaction to trauma, she asked me to move to the couch. We still had to do the heavy work of understanding the body's process. How it was doing what it was doing.

She never explained to me why she moved me to the couch, but I imagine that for the first few sessions it was crucial that I saw her face, noticed her body language and felt comfortable in that space. Once that comfort was established, I could, close my eyes and talk about everything without seeing her face, without trying to guess her responses, or without fearing judgment.

She started making me talk about how my child sexual abuse happened, in detail. It was on the couch that I cried for the first time in her office. It was on the couch that she made me see that what I thought was diarrhoea, was the purging of unwanted trauma. She asked me to visualise a sieve, and think of the entire trauma as the dirty, stinky water I had pushed out of my body that January night when I made the hospital visit. My bowel, we deduced, was that sieve. All the shit that my bowel had pushed out of my body was the trauma of rape and of a relationship on the verge of failure. The pain I was experiencing, physical and metaphorical, was my body trying to resist the letting go of what it knew so well. My body had been living with trauma for so long that without it, it would feel hollow and empty.

While I was in constant discomfort, my body, as it turned out, was healing. Of course, you can rubbish this theory. You could say that I was eating unhealthy food, not cooking for myself, being lazy and ordering take out, not working out and not sleeping on time. This unhealthy lifestyle was bound to have repercussions, and you would not be wrong. But my unhealthy lifestyle was also because of my past. I was fat because of my past. I was eating the way I was because I was often out of energy to cook. I was too unhappy to make efforts to build that energy.

When Zainab made me realise that my stomach had always been my problem area, it started to make sense. Because of the horrors of my past I was attuned to feeling things in the pit of my stomach, and my gut seldom lied. I relied on it, though I also acted against it.

One afternoon, when I was about ten or eleven, I was sitting in front of the television, the sofa chair pulled extremely close to the screen, with a big bowl of fryums in my hand, watching *Sholay*. My family was visiting a relative and I was alone at home. Suddenly I felt someone behind me, walking to the next room. The doors were locked from the inside and the possibility of an actual person walking behind me were close to none.

Since I believe in all forms of supernatural and paranormal things, my first thought was that it was a spirit. I immediately started reciting Our Father, the prayer taught to me by my hyper Christian school. In all the Hollywood horror films I had seen, the spirits were scared of the cross and prayers. As an upper caste Hindu in India, where minorities are routinely being pushed to the margins, the chances of a Christian prayer working for me were probably non-existent. I switched to the Hindu prayers Aai had taught me, but like any other kid who is a product of rote learning, I knew the words yet didn't know what they meant. No spirit was going to be fooled by my babble.

I decided to pay attention to *Sholay* instead; Jai and Veeru would save me. But that feeling that someone was lurking behind me did not leave. My parents and grandparents returned home in a few hours and I felt safe again. That night our house was robbed. I was convinced I had seen the thief through my bedroom window. Maybe I imagined him looking at me; my room was dark and it was almost impossible to see anything. But that feeling of immense dread I felt was anything but imaginary.

This is how my gut often works. It warns me that something bad is about to happen. If I don't trust it, something bad does happen. Another incident comes to mind. The year was 2000 and I was all of thirteen. It was our winter break and Aai and Baba decided to take us on a family vacation. This was the pre-ATM era. Back then, there were no cell phones. Men's underwear came with secret pockets to stash extra cash, as safeguard against pickpockets. Our destination was Tamil Nadu. There was no planning as such, we just took a train and arrived in Chennai. Baba had heard of a travel agency there and he thought it might be a good idea to get our itinerary planned by these experts.

Sitting in the office of that travel company, I began to get a bad feeling that something was not right with these people. But I was thirteen and didn't know how to trust myself, so I kept quiet. What a big mistake that was. That trip was a disaster. We were forced to stay in seedy hotels, eat terrible food, and travel in rickety buses. The worst was when we were in Kodaikanal. It was a beautiful hill station, all misty and cold, like they showed in the movies. It almost made us forget about the bad hotel we were staying in. On our last night in Kodaikanal I fell sick with terrible food poisoning.

Since we were tied to the travel agency's schedule, we had to leave for Madurai the next morning. We were tight on cash with no immediate means of withdrawing more money. Baba gave me meds and we hopped on our bus. I threw up all the way from Kodaikanal to Madurai, for four hours straight. In Madurai I was taken to a doctor and put on a drip. If the bad hotels, bad food, bad buses hadn't ruined things for us, the non-stop puke-fest certainly did.

The next day, we missed our train from Chennai that was supposed to end this nightmare of a journey and take us back home. We booked another train, this time to Nagpur, spent an extra day there with relatives, and took the bus to Jabalpur, officially ending the worst holiday of all our lives. Back home, I told Aai about the ill-feeling I had had at the travel agent's office. She was appalled that I hadn't said anything. I don't know if my speaking up would have made any difference. It was an unsubstantiated 'feeling' after all and nothing more. And I am not sure I had learned anything about trusting my gut from that episode either. I still don't trust my gut as often as I should.

When I told these things to Zainab, she told me that it appeared that my stomach was where I kept my anxieties. It was more attuned to the changes in the energies of my surroundings and was the first to respond to things. It explained why I got frequent stomach upsets and why, no matter what the illness, my digestive system was always the first to get affected. When she laid these thoughts out for me, I felt like someone had opened a knot in my stomach. It suddenly started making sense. I didn't need to be afraid of the stomach troubles anymore. My body was fighting for itself and not against me.

I needed to support it, listen to it, and not be afraid of it. It was scared of letting go of all the trauma and toxic associations I had built up over the years. I am still learning things about myself and the process seems long. But my fear of stomach troubles did slowly dissipate after I started seeing Zainab. I didn't know why it was happening, but my subconscious mind did.

When we talked about Avi, she listened to me carefully. After my past experience with therapy, I was hesitant. What if she considered my concerns frivolous? Like Avi's demand that I pick him up at the airport every single time. Or the fact that he did not like meeting people, and I was the only real person he relied on all the time. All I knew was that these things bothered me. Zainab helped me understand my irritation better. She asked me what I did when I was bothered by his behaviour. I told her I went to my friends and whined about things. She said I was able to whine about things to my friends because I had friends. If each time I went to Avi with all my problems then the relationship would not have survived even the first year of togetherness. Humans, she said, are social animals for a reason. We have our parents, cousins, friends, colleagues and lovers. People who understand us in different ways, and cater to our different needs. One person alone cannot play all roles or fulfil all our needs.

If we don't divide our energies and our expectations, the one person we are making all our demands of is bound to suffer. And so, she said, you are suffering. It took me a while to absorb her words, but I ultimately did. That year I summoned the courage to tell Avi that I needed physical distance from him. With Zainab's encouragement I told Avi I would be moving out and living with a friend for at least a few months. As I had expected, he didn't take it very well and acted like I was abandoning him. We had many fights.

I had friends who supported me throughout that phase and I had Zainab, but not for long. She had decided to pursue a PhD at Columbia University. My therapy sessions, after a meaningful run of seven months, came to an abrupt end. But I had already benefitted enough from our sessions. In August 2016, I moved out of the house we had shared in Delhi. I didn't know what it would ultimately mean for our relationship, but back then we were still going somewhat steady.

Avi would often resort to rage, brood and behave like a hurt and misunderstood puppy. But I was now strong enough to not give in to my urges to mother him. He was still one of the few people I relied on during my panic episodes, but living separately did make me feel better about myself. We lived apart for six months and with each day of that six-month period, the realisation that I wanted to end things with him kept getting stronger.

I stopped saying 'I love you,' to him, it was possible that he noticed it but didn't say anything, however the frequency of him verbalising his affection had increased. It felt dishonest. I could no longer show the affection I had once felt for him, and that had come naturally to me. I had been preparing for this for the past year and a half by having constant mental conversations. But now I was almost desperate to do it. I went home for Diwali that year and stayed home for two months. By this time I was ready to end my over four-year-long relationship.

At home I prepared myself. I wrote several drafts of the letter I was going to hand-deliver to him. I made sure I wasn't being harsh. I did not want to blame him for the failure of our relationship. And I didn't see it as a failure either. It was something that had just lived its full life. Parts of it were painful, but there had also been bits that were beautiful. It was the beauty I wanted to remember. I sent the letter to close friends, made them proof it for kindness.

How To Go Through A Breakup

Aaj Jaane Ki Zid Na Karo
–Fayyaz Hashmi

Before you begin to promise each
other that this love is eternal,
before you hold each other's hand
and sing, hopefully in the voice of
Farida Khannum, today, leave your
obstinance outside the door, today don't
leave me alone, think of all the things
you haven't said first.

Poetry cannot save you, dear child.
Not in this world of sorrow so out of
sync, all rhythm is lost on it. There is
no music in your sadness, what good
are you in this house of hollowed out
bones that are turning to mulch? Fodder
for another happy ending, just not yours.

Now, you begin by tearing down the
honeyed walls of your house.
You kill all spiders of thought
by bitter words of estrangement,
anger.

You think of the empty book shelves
that were going to be occupied
the year that never came to pass.
What lives there now are songs
 of resentment. Old boys standing
outside the house, watching it being
shredded to pieces. We do put up a
good show, don't we?

The ghosts that sat in empty corners,
have vacated the house. It is time
for us to do the same.
No matter what Pink Floyd says,
I do not wish you were here.
Today I don't choose you and
you don't choose me.
We are stray animals of this
starry night, lonely alligators from
a Lorca poem, but we don't share
the same sky anymore.

The scaffolding of memory is slowly
dissolving. There isn't much there
to hold on to. If I leave it, I leave you.
And I do. The house was
never ours anyway. The good thing
about being a tenant is the impermanency
of love. Today it's there, tomorrow it's gone.

Yes it was love, and yes it didn't last.
All the unreturned phone calls, and half-hearted
kisses, all the words of empty love,
everything that remains, remains undone.
Sometimes, it is better to bring your obstinance
inside. Sometimes it's better to just leave
me alone. Which is why, which is only why,
Aaj tum jaane ki zid karo.

When the time came to return to Delhi, I decided not to tell
him. The thought of doing something without informing him
made me feel anxious and guilty. Almost as if I was cheating
on him. But if I told him about my return, he would have
insisted on coming to the airport and I just could not have
that. It would make me weak.

I feel the anxiety of that moment even today, as I write
these lines and share with you my most private and painful
moments. On the 14 January 2017, I ended my relationship
with Avi. A mutual friend, who had offered to help, took my
letter to him and stayed with him till he read it and absorbed
the shock of it.

When he was done reading the letter, she texted me to
come to the house. I was sitting and waiting anxiously inside
a café, and I left immediately. I had to be strong enough to
meet him and see the anger and resentment on his face. When
I came in, Avi hugged me. He insisted that I drink some chai.
I kept crying and apologising for leaving him. He didn't show

any anger and that left me puzzled. This was the first time in our four-year-long relationship that Avi made chai for me. But I couldn't drink it. I put the cup down and ran out of the house. Our love story had finally ended.

3

'Begin at the beginning,' the King said very gravely, 'and go on till you come to the end: then stop.'

—Lewis Carroll, *Alice in Wonderland*

AFTER I RUSHED OUT of Avi's house, I went to PVR Saket. It was one of our old hangouts, where we had made many memories. Oddly, it felt like the right place to go to, to gather myself before I could decide what to do next. I knew I didn't want to be alone, I felt too vulnerable. In all likelihood, I would have ended up calling Avi and undoing all the emotional labour I had done. I called Navni, who told me to wait for her. She would come and pick me up.

I sat on one of the benches, sobbing as I waited, and called another friend, Arjun Rajendran. During times of anxiety, panic, heartbreak, or any moment of emotional duress, I do not retreat within myself. After years of carrying trauma within, when I finally started talking about it, I realised what a relief it was. I could function much better when there were people I could lean on. Sometimes I wonder if I am being a burden on my friends, but over the years I have also worked hard at building a community of people who have similar struggles. It never is just one person taking all the burden, it is always a few people.

This is a system that works rather well, and keeps me sane. If I did not do that I would possibly go through spontaneous human combustion and be burned to ashes. It sometimes is a slippery slope though. Some friends have joked about me being their therapist and while I get the humour I would caution the reader against such habits. It is easy to confuse friendly advice for therapy but unless you have training, and no close emotional ties to the person seeking help, listen to them, give them advice, and encourage them to seek psychiatric help. There are limitations to how much we can help our friends and those limitations should be respected, no matter what.

Arjun talked to me, reassured me that it took a lot of strength to do what I had done, and that it was the right thing. He also told me that I could go back to Avi in a few months' time if I felt like I still loved him. Despite my grief at the breakup, I didn't want the option of going back to Avi. Love was never really a concern for me. I loved him in some capacity, and maybe I could learn to fall in love with him again. I would not be able to forgive or really forget all that I had gone through when I was with him. I didn't think it would be fair to keep that hope of going back to him alive.

Soon Navni arrived. I ran to her car, and huddled inside, started wailing again. She took me to her house. With my puffy red eyes, my mismatched clothes and dishevelled hair,

I am sure I looked like a cast member of the *Night of the Living Dead*. But I felt anything but dead. I had too many feelings, alive and kicking within—fear, anxiety, hatred for myself. I kept wondering why Avi had not lashed out at me. Why had he chosen this moment to show compassion? Did I make a mistake?

I spent two days at Navni's and mostly spent my time crying. The first night, I remember, was exceptionally tough. Thankfully, Navni was by my side and did not let me call Avi and mess things up. In those two days, I realised that my beloved Delhi had become an alien city for me. I could not live there any longer. I needed to get away from it. While Delhi was the place I grew up and came of age in, it was also the city that represented the life I had had with Avi. Automatically then, Delhi represented lost love, the love that I let go, that I could not hold on to. Delhi had turned into a chamber of anxiety for me. It had given me strange breathing patterns, it had given me endless nightmares. If I needed to rebuild my life I needed distance from it. I needed to live in a city I didn't hate. A city that hadn't betrayed me.

After two days at Navni's, I went back to my place. I informed my flatmate that I would be leaving Delhi for good. It was an impulsive decision but I had never been more sure of anything. I called my parents and informed them that I was coming back home. They didn't require any convincing, puzzled as they were with this sudden decision. I had always told them I'd like to come back home for a few months while I sorted out my life.

I booked my train ticket for the next week. I went to the university, collected my mark sheet, my degree, and other certificates, packed all my stuff, arranged for the movers and packers to take them, and I was done. Continuing my stay in Delhi felt impossible. I would run into him, I had too many options of meeting him at a moment's notice. I was in too much pain to keep those options open for myself. I had to do something big and impulsive to make the break look small in comparison; even if it meant upending the life I had built in Delhi. When I was busy packing things and writing to people so I'd have freelance work, I was too busy to feel much pain.

I spent the next couple of days with my friends. My last ladies' night in Delhi, my last meal at a favourite restaurant, my last time with every single person I knew in Delhi… I made my departure ceremonious. It was my final, final moment. I had to live it. I had to pay my final respects to the city. I could not have left it without saying all my goodbyes. I went to my regular haunts. I roamed around without purpose in Connaught Place and Hauz Khas Village. Saket would have been too painful or I would have liked to go to the garden in front of my former house at least once.

Soon enough it was time to leave. I boarded the train and cried through the night. My tryst with Delhi had ended, at least for the time being. When I reached home, it took me a few days to unwind and unpack. I organised my clothes, books, bags and shoes in their new place of residence. Unpacking and rearranging was the easy part of the healing process. Now that I was finally beginning to settle into my new old life, slowing down to match its pace was the thing that I had to form a habit of. I set camp in Aaji's room and chuckled at the jokes life keeps playing.

This incessant need life has to form a full circle. When I was growing up, our house was small. Always too many occupants and too few rooms. I was made to share a room with Aaji. Now that she was gone, I was still doing that. I was living in her room and sleeping on her bed. I chose the opposite side of the bed for myself and kept her spot vacant. The first thing I did when I moved into her room was scrub the bathroom clean. It was already sparkling clean, but it still smelled like her. I didn't want to smell her presence there. I changed the bedsheet, asked Aai to give me a new one. My new life deserved fresh bedsheets and pillowcases, and a bathroom that smelled like me, or if not me then the Godrej air freshener, just not Aaji. My new life had to be free of my past. Of all my pasts.

In 2017, the year I moved back home, I had thought I would piece together all the scattered, broken parts of me that I had collected, packed, and brought back with me. The hair pulling had not stopped but now I had Aai to constantly nag me about it. I had to hide it from her and that was not easy. She kept showing me the mirror and all the scars I had given myself. She and Baba already knew about how depressed and anxious I always was, but it was still difficult for them to understand why their perfectly raised, happy child had fallen into the hands of depression. They tried to be understanding and empathetic, and that was more than I could have asked for anyway.

In the last two years I had managed to form a lot of bad, unhealthy habits. I had overeaten my way to serious obesity. By the time I moved to Jabalpur, I weighed 96 kilos. I hardly moved. I would sleep all day, occasionally write poetry, binge watch TV shows and not talk to anyone. I mostly stayed confined to my room and preferred that loneliness to making futile conversation. Interacting with people required me to hide behind a happy façade and I found that exhausting. My room became my refuge.

One May morning I woke up feeling extremely dizzy. The world around me spun out of control for a few excruciatingly long seconds. When that stopped, nausea set in. I didn't throw up but wanted to, really badly, just to rid myself of that horrible feeling of vomit stuck in my throat. That whole day the feeling of dizziness continued. I was confused about what this could be. For the past two years I had been roaming around feeling disoriented. I had read up on it. Continuous disorientation was a result of anxious living. When your head is flooded with too many thoughts flowing at the same time, when your heart is pacing at an unexpectedly high rate, when you are losing a sense of your surroundings, finding it difficult to make decisions, when you feel like you might faint, you could have anxiety. Though you should get yourself checked for other things just in case. However, a little bit of self-diagnosis might take you to the doctor you need.

Feeling dizzy is also your body's response to anxiety. I

wasn't new to anxiety, in fact by then I was well-equipped to handle minor episodes. But this seemed more serious. I didn't tell anyone and continued with my day, hoping the dizziness would go away on its own, as it usually does with anxiety episodes. After three days, when it still persisted I had to tell Aai. She immediately launched an investigation. I had to get my complete blood tests done. Baba was convinced that this was a cervical issue. 'Is your neck hurting?' he asked. It wasn't and he was stumped out of a diagnosis.

A CBC test was ordered and it came back with all kinds of bad news. My blood sugar levels were high, haemoglobin levels were low, my cholesterol levels were haywire. Now, the real panic set in. I started crying, howling. I had managed to ruin my life completely. I hadn't even turned thirty and I already had been diagnosed with diabetes.

Aai booked an appointment with her doctor. He saw my reports, my body weight, and told me my life was officially over. Or he didn't, but to me it sounded like he did. I was prescribed pills and asked to start working out. My hypochondria related anxiety was already working overtime. I had, by now, imagined dying quietly of a heart attack—like the one that hits you mid-sleep and kills you. I had imagined dying like Shahrukh Khan in *Kal Ho Na Ho*, dancing my way to a heart failure.

There were other complications too, like kidney failure. Liver damage. Paralysis. Blindness. The biggest worry though was injuring my foot, it being infected, and then eventually being amputated. I lived with the extreme fear of amputation, so grave that I would get a panic attack if something fell even near my foot. The only positive aspect of my hypochondria was that it made me start working out seriously, and go on a diet. It is something I have always been against, politically, and still struggle to accept.

The first step towards healing came when I started going on walks. Aai and Baba, worried about their young daughter's morbidity, decided to take some serious action. We bought a treadmill. I got some weights. I started jogging, slowly but steadily. When the monsoons hit, I stepped out of the house and walked around the neighbourhood, welcoming the monsoon breeze. I would walk for five or six kilometres every day and jog for at least two of those six kilometres.

All the work outs and healthy eating had another unexpected benefit. They silently helped me ride the wave of depression that had taken over rather strongly after my diagnosis had come in. The exercise would release dopamine in my head and I would feel lighter, better, happier even. It made me more productive than I had been in a while. I wrote an essay on Trichotillomania which remains one of my most popular essays. It has been three years now and I still get messages from people, sharing their stories about how they have been harassed because of their missing eyebrows that they pulled out compulsively, or how they didn't even know what they did had a medical name, and how it has helped them feel a bit better, more courageous and less alone.

That year, for the first time in my life, I also wrote a long essay about my child sexual abuse experiences. One of my abusers, Ajit, was celebrating his fortieth birthday that year. His relative, who was still our next-door neighbour in Jabalpur, was making a video for him as a gift. A video where all his loved ones were to say wonderful, kind things about him, or recount some funny memory they remembered him by. He was, after all, a funny guy. The funniest guy.

'It's a lazy July afternoon. I am standing in the kitchen of our newly renovated house when my neighbour comes to me, asking if I have a little time. As I butter my toast, she talks. She tells me about a birthday surprise that has been planned for her brother-in-law. She wants me to say something nice about him—a fond memory, if I can recall any. I have several of those.

I once had a bet with him over a few guavas, my favourite fruit as a kid. He asked me to eat a spoonful of salt, and if I did that, I would get to take as many guavas from the tree in his backyard as I wanted. So, I ate a spoonful of salt, and was told I would get to take the guavas.

On the tree, as I tried plucking them, the smell of guavas that were ripe just the right amount was in the air, and there was a flood of saliva in my mouth. He climbed the tree to help me, and it was the first time I felt something poking me hard from behind. It was strange, it hurt a little, it was confusing, and it was also exciting. The guavas fell from my hand, and I didn't ever climb that tree again.'

The thought of having to say nice things about my abuser unsettled me and that is what propelled me to write my essay. Of course, no one knew what he had done, but it still didn't feel fair. Since I could not cry about this to anyone in my family, I wrote about it. I pitched the essay to Buzzfeed India. Their then commissioning editor excitedly accepted the essay, then got busy for months and didn't write back to me for a long time. When he finally did, he sent a somewhat butchered essay back for me to take a look.

This broke my heart. When I had sent the pitch for the essay I had asked about the word count and was informed that the essay could be as long as 3000 words. The initial feedback I was given was that there might be some minor edits. In my years as a writer I have learned a lot from good editors. I am very open to edits and feedback and I know when to keep my writer's ego aside. But this case was different. It was a highly personal essay that was 2700 words long, and when I got it back it had been cut down to 1100 words. There were no notes, no explanations offered on why that had happened. To this day, that remains the only essay I withdrew from publication. The money was great, but this wasn't an essay I had written for money.

I was disappointed and broken. *The first time I write about my darkest experiences, and the world humiliates me*, I thought. I then wrote to another editor who is now a dear friend, Shreya Ila Anusuya, who edited *Skin Stories*, an online space for writings on disability and sexuality. She accepted my essay. It was more than twice the size of what they usually published but she still accepted it, offered some notes on how to edit and make it better, and published my piece after I had worked on it.

My story was out in the world, for everyone to read. When

it came out I was in Kasauli, holidaying with two friends. This was the first time I was away from home since my diagnosis. Aai was worried sick. But I was happy because despite all my fears I was able to function well. I had also lost ten kilos and felt fitter. My sugar levels were under control too.

When I reached home, the doctor advised I take the HBA1C test. For those who are lucky enough to not know what that is, HBA1C or Glycated haemoglobin is a test that tells you how your sugar levels have fared in the last three-four months. For a non-diabetic the normal range of Haemoglobin A1C is between 4–5.9 per cent. This time my readings were well under 5.5 per cent. Even if this was a temporary development, I was on my way to reversing my diabetes. Till this point I was taking Metformin 500 twice a day. With the new results, the doctor changed my dosage to once a day. That month I started doing strength training along with my brisk walk. Jillian Michaels of *The Biggest Loser* fame came into my life. I was enjoying working out, if not her abuses, and that helped my metabolism tremendously.

I was never able to diet with much success, and while I stuck to eating healthy most days, my portion sizes had gone down considerably, though with occasional indulgences. But with the new workout routine, controlled eating and Metformin that I was taking daily, my sugar levels would often fall below normal levels. I was asked to stop taking meds completely and introduce some amount of sugar in my diet, even one tiny cube of chocolate would do.

Within five months of my diagnosis I had managed to

bring my situation under control. That year I also applied to a writing residency in Finland, called the Villa Sarkia Writing Residency. I was chosen and started preparing for my stay in Finland. The year 2017 had started on a low note. I had ended my four-year-long relationship in January, and been diagnosed with a chronic illness only a few months later, but by the end of the year, I had managed to dramatically improve my health. Now, I was preparing for my first international trip. And I had been invited to my first literary festival to read my poems and talk about my mental health journey.

After all, diabetes wasn't the worst thing to have happened to me.

At the start of 2018, I went to Delhi to get my visa work done for Finland. I was nervous about the paperwork and the interview, never having travelled anywhere abroad. But Europe is no America and I got the visa work done within half an hour, being the only person applying for a Finnish visa that day. It was a warm winter. The impact of climate change was ruining the one thing about Delhi that set it apart—its winters. I was staying at Navni's, my usual place to crash when in Delhi. Avi and I had not lost touch, I would meet him whenever I'd be in Delhi, and this time was no different, but staying at his place felt hard. Especially since I had tried it once and it caused me a tremendous amount of anxiety, one that made me break a brand new bottle of wine.

Nothing could dampen my spirits though. Now that my paperwork was done, and I was pretty sure I was going to get my visa approved, I knew I was going to fly out of the country for my first international trip soon. I was feeling a little brave already. From Delhi I was flying straight to Mumbai for the newly instated and now (probably) defunct Bandra Literary Festival. A lot of my close poet friends were gathering there.

In 2016, poet Nandini Dhar, who I consider a mentor and also a close friend, had invited me to join a poetry project that she and another poet, Mihir Vatsa, were working on. Mihir and Nandini both run literary journals *Vayavya* and *Aaina Nagar*, respectively. The two journals had come together to work on a poetry project that aimed at bringing together five Indian poets, and publishing five chapbooks of poetry that would be put in a box and sold together. The idea was to encourage new voices and independent publishing, and to promote the idea of a literary community. You could only buy the chapbooks as a collection, no one poet's work would be sold separately. One for all, all for one.

When Nandini invited me to join the project, I was enthralled. I was always looking for a community of writers to learn from, and this was my big chance. I remember jumping at the opportunity. Arjun, another poet and the friend I had called soon after my breakup, was also a part of the project. And Usha Akela, a diaspora poet whose work I was familiar with. It was a small, but interesting group. Over the course of two years I read everyone's chapbook, I critiqued their work as they critiqued mine. I learned not just about poetry, but also how to appreciate and criticise other people's works. After two years of that labour, the chapbooks were finally ready and looking gorgeous.

At the Bandra Literary Festival we launched the chapbooks. We were each to read some of our poems and talk about our takeaways from this project. I was nervous, something everyone could see, but by the time I was done with the first reading I had calmed down. The next day, the organiser of the festival requested me to read a few more poems, since they were one participant short. I had no time to mentally prepare for it, but I looked up a few of my old poems on the phone, and read them, with much more confidence than I had exhibited the first time.

Finally, on the last day of the festival, I was a part of a mental health panel, where I was supposed to read a few poems about my struggles with depression. I did that, but also decided to talk a little about it. I spoke of my child sexual abuse, I discussed its lingering effects on me even today, how PTSD works and how literature has helped me. It was a very movie-like moment. I had no speech prepared, but I still gave one. The panel was a success. My first literary event, and I didn't make a fool of myself, despite serious anxiety. I was proud of myself and felt pretty awesome. This year was going to be a great one.

I left for home the next day. January was almost over. I was to fly to Helsinki on 28 February and spend the next two months in a small Finnish village called Sysmä. I bought a lot of warm clothes and a pair of sturdy yet sexy looking boots. My visa arrived and soon it was time to leave for Mumbai again to catch my flight. Until I reached Mumbai, I was in denial of my anxiety, though I could feel it slowly gathering in my stomach like an impending storm.

It would hit me properly only on the day of my departure. In Mumbai, I was staying with my brother Mrugank, whom we call Golu at home. His house was in Madh Island in those days. Travelling from Madh is quite annoying because getting cabs is hard. And it does not help that the island is a good 26 km away from the airport. There was a ferry that would take you to mainland Mumbai—Versova, but it only worked till 1 a.m. And there was no guarantee you'd find an auto that late in the night, so my brother suggested we take the ferry at around 10, when there were still autos in sight. We took an auto to the ferry. We set sail at 10 p.m. for a 5.30 a.m. flight. We called a cab to the airport upon reaching the Versova village and were there by 10.45 p.m.

While in the cab, I kept wondering if I could still cancel my plans. I would lose close to forty thousand rupees that I had spent from my savings on the tickets and visa, but it was my money, right? I could make that money again. My middle-class mind was conflicted. Waves of nausea were hitting me. I was constantly on the verge of tears in the cab. Aai had made sure Golu accompanied me to the airport. He played his part well, patting my head and trying to comfort me. We reached the airport, he hugged me and asked me to take care of myself, and reassured me that nothing bad was going to happen. I was going to have a great time.

So far I had been trying to fight back tears, but the moment I stepped inside the airport I burst out crying. I found myself a somewhat empty corner and sobbed. When I felt I could cry no more, I dragged my luggage to the washroom, threw up, popped a medicine for nausea and anxiety, and drank a lot of water. I went to find out when they'd be opening the check-in counters for my flight. They looked at me like I was some mad woman, with bloodshot eyes, wet cheeks from all the crying and probably vomit breath. The woman there told me the check-in would start after 2.30 a.m. It was only 11 pm. I had a lot of time to kill.

After some time, the Clonazepam settled in my system and I finally felt a bit relaxed. I found myself a spot and opened one of the six books I was carrying. My first Jeanette Winterson, *Why Be Happy When You Could Be Normal.*

At the airport, as I waited for the check-in counter to open, I finished reading the first chapter, clicked pictures of myself and of passages from the book, shared those and put up a post about my anxiety, asking people for tips. A lot of people responded. Someone asked me to chug some alcohol. Another person asked me to take my anxiety medicine and practise deep breathing. Someone suggested I make a list. Someone asked me to read poetry.

I took out all my travel documents, clicked pictures and sent them to friends. I, then, made a list of phone numbers that might come handy in case I lost my phone and stuffed copies of these numbers in every piece of luggage I owned. I took out my medicine pouch and moved it to a more accessible place. I plugged in my earphones, set an alarm for 30 minutes later and took a disjointed nap. Soon, but not soon enough, it was time to check myself in.

I had skipped dinner because I was too anxious to eat and

my stomach rumbled in hunger, but the thought of food made me nauseous and reminded me of the throwing up I had done only a few hours back. Trying to think of something else, I grabbed myself a coffee and waited for the boarding to begin. A couple of hours later, I was on the plane. Fourteen hours, and one long layover at Istanbul later, I was in Helsinki.

Despite all the preparation, I had still forgotten to keep a coat in my hand luggage. I had just one sweater on me, which was pretty useless in −21 degrees weather. I didn't have the energy to open my suitcase and take out a coat, so I decided to brave the cold. The airport had a subway station within it but it was approximately a kilometre away. I had two giant suitcases and one backpack. I could have taken a cab to my bed and breakfast, but that would mean spending 50 euros, something I didn't want to do. I decided to walk instead. When I reached the subway, I stood in front of the escalator, wondering how to carry all this luggage on it. It struck me that I am in a first world country. If the Delhi metro has a lift, Helsinki metro has to have one too. A kind man came to me and asked if I'd like him to help me with my luggage. I was still adjusting to this new surrounding and didn't feel safe to accept his help. Instead I asked him if there was a lift nearby and he pointed me to it, I thanked him and took the lift.

When I got to the platform I realised that all the signs were in Finnish. I didn't know which train to take because I couldn't read the language. I spotted the same guy who'd helped me. Looking at my puzzled expression, he came up to me again and offered help. This time, I accepted. I asked him about which train to take and he told me he was going my way and I should take the same train as him. When the train arrived, he helped me put my luggage inside and asked me my name. 'Manjiri,' I said, and he tried to pronounce it. MANjeeree? Marjoree? MANjri? 'Sure,' I said to the last one, it was close enough. My postcolonial brain found his attempts adorable. His name was Phillipe and he introduced me to his friend who was with him, whose name I don't remember anymore.

When we reached the next station, Phillipe realised that he had made me take the wrong train. He asked me to not panic, got off the train with me, telling his friend he'd first drop me off at the right stop and then head home. My head was buzzing with suspicious thoughts. What would Aai say if she found out I was letting a stranger take me to a station whose name I couldn't even read? What if he took me to the wrong place? What if he robbed me, or worse, raped me and then robbed me? While these morbid thoughts buzzed in my head, Phillipe kept making polite conversation.

He was a chef at one of the Finnish cuisine restaurants at the airport. He was half Italian and half Cuban. He had been living in Finland for over two decades. He asked me if I liked to dance. He was a good dancer, he said. He wanted to know if I'd like to experience the night life of Helsinki. He could take me out when I had settled in and was not jet lagged. And he wanted to know if I would be interested in giving him my number.

I lied through my teeth and said I was yet to open the SIM

package and install it on my phone. Why didn't he give me his number, I proposed. I'd buzz him when my phone was functional. He gave me his number. I told him I wouldn't be staying in Helsinki the next day as I was headed to Sysmä, on a writing residency. He looked impressed.

When my station finally arrived, he again helped me with my luggage, hugged me goodbye, and went on his way. I had managed to get asked out on a date as soon as I landed in Finland. Usually I would have felt validated, but back then I was too anxious to feel anything other than cold. With my obsession with romantic movies, I could've made this my big romantic comedy moment, but I let it slip away. I could have given him my number, or asked him to walk with me to my BnB. Maybe we could've talked all night? But I chose anxiety over romance. I let him go.

I reached the BnB and made some soup for myself, my first meal in over 30 hours. I took a shower and finally went to bed. I woke up early the next day. I explored the house I was staying in, it was beautiful and super neat. No matter how far you looked, all you could see from the windows were snow-covered roads and roofs. And no people. I stepped outside to feel the freezing cold breeze and click some pictures. I did that for about a minute before rushing back to the warmth of the house.

I had an 11 a.m. bus to catch that would take me to Sysmä. I scrounged the BnB kitchen and finally found some oats and tea bags, which I used for breakfast. Soon enough I was on the bus. It was a three-hour drive. When I reached, the coordinator of the residency was waiting for me at the bus stand. She took me to the house I was going to be staying in.

It was big and beautiful. It had a big wooden porch with two benches for sitting outside, though it felt impossible in this weather. There was also a huge garden but it was all snowed in. The snow cover was almost knee-deep. There were benches in the garden when one could have their breakfast in better weather. For now, it was all sheathed in white and looked isolated yet beautiful.

When I entered the house I was greeted by two of my housemates, Yolanda and Heidi. Yolanda was originally from Spain but lived in Germany, and Heidi was from Finland. The village she grew up in was an hour away from where we were, just across the lake that was almost 500 metres away from the house. She, too, lived in Germany now. They had cooked some Spanish rice with saffron for me. They told me they were stepping out for a bit and I should eat something, since I looked tired.

I dumped my luggage in my room, changed into something comfortable, and gratefully ate the rice. When I was sitting at the airport in Mumbai, I had been worrying about the cold weather in Finland. I didn't know how to deal with such low temperatures, what if my body was not able to cope with the cold? The worries came rushing back. To make myself feel better I wrote in my journal, 'You don't have to leave the house if you don't want to. There is no pressure of such a performance on you.'

When I was done eating, a wave of extreme loneliness hit

me. I didn't know what to do. After lunch the first thing I did was unpack my stuff and organise the room the way I liked. That kept me occupied for almost an hour, but the second that was done, the feeling of loneliness was back. By this time, both my housemates were back too. Heidi asked me if I wanted to go to the grocery store to get some supplies for myself. She said it was okay if I was tired, I could do it the next day. The house had enough supplies. And I was carrying several packets of Knorr soups, Maggi, and Masala Oats anyway.

My loneliness pushed me towards accepting her offer. I changed into my jeans, wore my warm clothes, ear muffs, and my scarf, and was soon walking in the snow with Heidi. This would turn out to be my most visited place in this village and I would soon master this route. At the supermarket I bought a lot of vegetables, rice, some pasta, some fruits, some biscuits, milk, eggs and cereal. I picked out the cheapest of all available options. I felt good and rather responsible. As we walked back home, Heidi showed me the way to the nearby flea markets, restaurants and bars if I wanted to go. I knew I wouldn't be doing that. I was saving up money for Helsinki.

I came back home and decided to explore the house. My housemates had told me that traditionally all Finnish houses have saunas. I jumped a little with joy when I realised this one did too. Heidi explained to me how it was therapeutic, how it released all the toxins from your skin, and was a calming and meditative space. She taught me how to work the sauna and that evening I went downstairs and sat inside the steamy chamber for my first sauna experience. Afterwards I took a shower, chopped some vegetables, made a quick salad for myself, had it and slept.

Next morning I woke up at six—I was still on India time—and that minor jetlag was actually helpful. I freshened up, wore my comfy woollen indoor boots, picked up Jeanette, my laptop, pen, journal and meds, and went downstairs. The living room was big and white, with large windows and larger bookshelves, crowded mostly with books in Finnish. It had an old, sturdy dining table and chairs. It had a television and a big, comfortable couch, and a centre table right next to it. Everyone else seemed to be sleeping, so I cat-footed my way to the kitchen and made some adrak ki chai for myself. Aai had made sure to pack some spices like cardamom and clove in my bag, I grated some ginger, I put all the spices, and my chai, which would soon enough be called chai-tea by my housemates, was ready.

I grabbed a couple of biscuits I had bought the previous day, and my giant mug of tea, went to the living room, plopped myself on the sofa and started reading *Why Be Happy...*I read some and then scribbled something in my diary. By this time everyone was up in the house and it was time for breakfast. I got up, washed my mug and the pot I had made tea in, took a bowl, poured some cereal in it, cut a fruit and added it to my cereal along with some yoghurt. The first bite I took of my cheapest, no-sugar cereal felt wholesome, like a symphony melting in my mouth. The pear, the most boring fruit, a fruit I avoid eating in India, that I had only bought because it was the cheapest of the available options, was so beautiful that I could have cried. That day I had my breakfast with my housemates. Then I went back to my laptop and started writing. I had an essay due for the *Indian Express*.

Waking up at six, tea and biscuits with Jeanette, breakfast—mostly alone—and then writing for hours became my routine in the house. I joined a gym nearby, where I would go for a swim. In the evenings, I would go for a walk on the frozen lake and would pick up my groceries for the next few days on my way back. At night I would go and sit in the sauna. This would be my day.

Heaven is the Place of Unprecedented Happiness

I live in a village of no visitors.
When passersby look at me, they wonder:
what got her here? A little boy asks me
why I am wearing the coat of anxiety
in this wintry weather of frothy happiness.
People here call my morning chai,
chai tea, and I hear Aaji laughing at me,
as if saying, it serves me right to travel to this
land of no returns without her. You see, I locked
my doors for her. I showed her the sign that read
ENTER ONLY IF MADNESS PERMITS.
Don't get me wrong, she was mad.
And madness would permit. But I, her clever
grandchild, also knew she would not permit madness
to permit her entry. She was a complicated fool.
Like me.

So, the doors are shut, and I am stuck in Santa Claus's
village. Mrs Claus brings me hot cocoa which has been
over sugared. For she knows what others don't.
Too much sugar will rot your soul.
There are beautiful lights in this village.
Empty carousels of death spin in circles making me
dizzy. When I vomit here, I vomit rainbows.
And Aai reminds me to clean up the mess I
leave behind. No matter where you are, don't
forget your manners. When they kill you,
don't spill too much blood. It's a mess she
won't come to clean.

I went for a walk yesterday, the loneliness
of this house made me long for the loneliness
of the streets. This time, I left behind my coat
of anxiety. I wore the borrowed scarf of depression.
I knew it would keep me warm the way
only depression can. It keeps me one with the
outside calm. A sign reads in Finnish, *Beware
of the Icicles*. But I can't read it. So, I stand underneath
one, to see if one will fall on me, penetrate my skull.
The boy is back again. This time riding a sledge.
He offers me a ride to the village where toys
are made. He's the manager there. He can offer
me a job of manufacturing happiness for the
already happy. So, I say to him, *why not?*
And hop on his sledge.

The landscape is new now. Happiness is injected
inside candies and you are forced to take one each
day. Aaji greets me at the reception, says: Welcome
to heaven, the place of unprecedented happiness.
You'll love it here. It's a slogan that flashes all around
this village. They've forced all my sadness out of me.
It's illegal to be anything but happy here. I fear jail
time, where they force you to drink too much hot
chocolate, till it burns your tongue.
Now, I can finally say,
I am happy, happy, happy.
Yes, yes.
I am happy, happy, happy.
Thank you for asking.

This was the first poem I wrote in Finland. I was so lonely
in that lovely house. Yet, I was also happy and productive. I
would have depressive episodes wherein I would panic and
call up friends. The next day I would recover from those
and resume my routine. I wrote a few essays when I was
there. I wrote a lot of poems. I went to a nearby city called
Lakhti, explored the whole city on foot, all its museums, all
the churches, all the flea markets. Heidi had introduced me
to a friend of hers who met me for lunch and then we both
shopped together. That day I got to see a lot of people and it
made me realise how much I had missed the noise, the hustle
and bustle. What a difference seeing people could make to
my mood.

Living in India, you never want for noise. From your loud neighbour's blaring TV to the vegetable vendor, from the domestic helps and their incessant chatter with your mother to honking automobiles on the streets, to the unruly children whose kites somehow always land on your terrace, there are always noises. These sounds are such an essential part of your life, you don't even realise it, till you're actually in a place which is quiet. In Finland, I had to develop a routine for myself so I could have some noise in the house, be it in the form of music or reruns of shows I liked. It was the only way I could survive the loneliness I felt. And it wasn't the loneliness that the place was subjecting me to, it was my own loneliness, the one that I had carried within myself from my home country, that I had the luxury to deny when I was at home, in my safe space.

Walking around in Lakhti, talking to the people in those museums and churches, and almost sitting in for an alcoholics anonymous meeting, that was happening in the basement of the church—a woman confused me for a fellow alcoholic and asked me if I would be joining in. I fought the temptation hard and ultimately could not bring myself to disrespect people and their struggles, however lonely I felt—I was desperate for human contact.

Soon enough my days in Finland came to an end and it was time to go home. I packed my bags and left for Helsinki. I reached my BnB, dumped my things and left for the city centre. Again I explored all the museums, enjoyed some Finnish gothic rock music and went to more churches. I grabbed a bite to eat before returning to my BnB which had a beautiful cat called Pulla, which is the name for Finnish cardamom bread. The cat and I chilled a lot when I was in her house. I fell asleep cuddling with the cat.

I flew back the next day. I returned home in the second week of April. I had lost weight in Finland. Every day walks and swims in the cold weather, and just eating raw veggies and cereal out of laziness was bound to do that. My skin was glowing. My hair was shining. I was feeling good. At the end of my residency a popular literary agent, whose name you might be familiar with, Kanishka Gupta, wrote to me asking if I'd ever thought about writing a book on living with depression and anxiety.

I had thought about it, just not seriously enough to pursue it. He asked me to consider it and said he would like to represent me. I thought about it, and said yes. Soon enough a proposal was drafted, sent out to publishers, and was picked by the publisher whose name sits on the cover of my book. The year 2018 was when things turned around for me.

It wasn't like I was cured of my depression. It wasn't like my anxiety had vanished. It wasn't like I had lost all that extra weight, or I had become super healthy. But things were looking up. That year I went to Bangalore in August to attend the Bangalore Poetry Festival. I stayed with a new friend I had met on Facebook a few months back and immediately bonded with over a shared love for Bollywood, and fell in love. I spoke in front of a large audience and was appreciated. Anxiety be damned, I was finally myself.

Writing this book has been one tough journey for me. I had to live through a lot of difficult memories, things I had pushed aside, things I had locked inside dark cupboards. As these memories resurfaced, many realisations also happened. I kept telling people to not put themselves through this process of writing memoirs, it yields no good results, but the truth is that this book turned my life around for me. Today, I am a different person than I was when I started writing this book. Today I am able to demand my space better because I am able to understand and empathise with my struggles better.

When I ended things with Avi I was not able to cut ties with him entirely. In 2019, I finally did that. And I would like to believe I did it with empathy, that I did what was best for him. But more importantly, I did it for myself. In 2019, I started therapy once again. In 2019, I told my parents about my child sexual abuse experiences and we all survived it. In 2019, I decided to fall in love again. And I hope by the time I get ready to write my next book I will have found love.

The King had asked Alice to go on till the end and then stop. This, by no means is the end of my story. But I am choosing to stop here for now.

Until we meet again.

Acknowledgements

IT TAKES A VILLAGE to raise a child, they say. This child of mine took a whole city. My parents, who were endlessly supportive despite my tantrums, my sleeplessness invoked grumpiness, my rage and emotional imbalances, and my moody fits. Had they not been patient and kind and ever encouraging, I'd never have finished this book. My brother Mrugank for being my support system within the family and helping me get through the exhausting process of writing this book.

Rheea Mukherjee for reading this book closely, giving me brutally honest feedback, and not letting me stray. Nandini Dhar for always being ready to read my chapters and seeing things I missed with her critical and sharp eyes. Shreya Ila Anusuya who published the essays in the journal she edits, *Skin Stories*, that ultimately led to this book. Navni Kumar for being the shoulder I always cried on when I was tired of writing things I never thought I'd be writing.

Sanghamitra Biswas for being the dream editor and friend, who pointed out critically but kindly all my gaffes, and also made this entire grilling process rewarding and fun. My always supportive agent and friend Kanishka Gupta for showing faith in my work, and not giving up on me. Sadaf Basheer Vidha, my therapist for providing me with the safe space I needed to keep going.

Bollywood—had it not been for cinema I would not have made it out alive, I would not be the person I am. And finally, to all survivors of sexual abuse who wrote to me upon reading my essays and Facebook posts. It was your strength, courage, and support above everything else that helped me reach the finish line.

For helping me cope, live, and thrive, thank you.

Made in the USA
Coppell, TX
10 November 2020